Dennis,

Nice Meeting [...]

M000044285

Mark

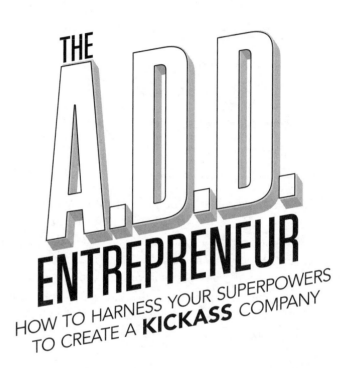

THE A.D.D. ENTREPRENEUR

HOW TO HARNESS YOUR SUPERPOWERS TO CREATE A **KICKASS** COMPANY

By

Matt Curry

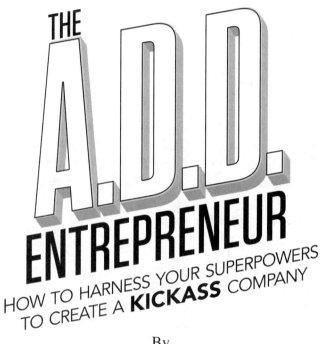

With Foreword by
Cameron Herold

Bestselling Author of
*Double Double:
How to Double Your Revenue
and Profit in Three Years or Less*

To my parents, Bill and Claire Curry; my wife, Judy; and our children Matthew and Jenna. For the loving support of my brothers and sisters, Susan, Linda, Bill, Bob, Kathy and Dianne. Thank you for keeping me grounded and letting me soar. You are my inspiration.

Also, to all the budding entrepreneurs (with or without A.D.D.) and to all the Mavericks out there (you know who you are!): Keep on doing what you do. The world needs you now more than ever.

CONTENTS

FOREWORD

Matt has written a book that needs to be read. Not by everyone – but it needs to be read by all entrepreneurs and their employees, and I'd even suggest it should be read by those telling entrepreneurs to "conform" to be more like them.

Entrepreneurs are different. We're wired differently. We're the 1%. To others, we're on the lunatic fringe, and to many, we're risk takers. However, when you get a group of entrepreneurs in a room together, we're pretty much all the same. One of the key traits that makes us who we are is that most of us "suffer" from Attention Deficit Disorder (A.D.D.).

The big "aha" I had years ago was that we don't actually suffer from A.D.D. What we suffer from is "professionals" like teachers and doctors telling us that we have a problem when in fact, A.D.D. doesn't have to be a problem at all. It's one of the key things that makes us successful as an entrepreneur.

Think of it this way: it's like a glass of water that's half filled up. It's either half full or half empty. To the thirsty person, that glass of water is a gift they get to enjoy. A.D.D. is quite similar. To teachers and doctors, it's a problem because all they see and focus on are the negatives. However, as entrepreneurs, we actually benefit from having A.D.D. It allows us to see all the things related to our business that others miss – like the market, customers, employees, financials, product, etc. – except we don't hyper-focus on what we see. We can't. We have A.D.D.

Because we see everything, we have the big picture. And because we can't focus on stuff very well for a long period of time, we end up hiring others to do that for us. Ah... delegation! See, A.D.D. has us as entrepreneurs starting things, getting a little bored, and passing it off to others. That's precisely what you need to do if you want to start and grow companies.

Matt's book outlines some of the tips to leveraging A.D.D. And as all of us who have it know, we want the short cuts; we want the easy solutions. His book gives them to us.

Protect your confidence as an entrepreneur, and leverage your strengths. Perhaps A.D.D. is actually a strength, and perhaps the "disease" is really the medical community and school systems telling us and our parents that there was something wrong with us. A.D.D. is only a disorder to the people in the middle, the followers. You're not supposed to be like teachers and doctors, and they're not supposed to be like you. You're not a follower.

You're an entrepreneur. Entrepreneurs are wired differently. Embrace that, and grow. Matt's book will give you the inspiration to do it.

Cameron Herold
CEO Coach and Bestselling Author of:
Double Double: How to Double Your Revenue and Profit in Three Years or Less

INTRODUCTION

My name is Matt, but some people have called me HazMat, which is short for "hazardous material." My wife, Judy, says she's the Tasmanian Devil Whisperer. That's because I have a condition called Attention Deficit Disorder, commonly known as A.D.D. or A.D.H.D. My A.D.D. makes it really hard (OK, impossible…) for me to sit still and focus on anything for more than a few minutes. I'm like a pinball, bouncing off the walls, switching gears on a dime. My mind and body go full tilt from the moment I wake up in the morning until I finally fall asleep at night. Life is kind of crazy for me sometimes.

I was diagnosed with A.D.D. back in the 1970s, when I was eleven years old. I always got along great with the other kids in school, but as I grew older, my non-stop energy became harder for me and my teachers to manage. Consequently, my grades weren't very good. I was getting low B's and C's even though everybody told me I was smart enough to earn A's. Unless I was doing something I enjoyed and appreciated, I had trouble sitting still and staying on task, not only at school, but also when it came time to do my homework and other activities. My parents were worried about me, so they took me to Massachusetts General Hospital in Boston for testing during summer vacation between the sixth and seventh grades. I had no idea why I was there. I didn't think there was anything wrong with me. I was happy. I was involved in sports, and I had lots of friends. Life was good from my perspective.

But the doctors at Mass General believed my life could be better. They diagnosed me with A.D.D. and prescribed a drug called

Ritalin, which had recently been approved to treat children with my condition. I was a "Ritalin Baby," one of the first guinea pig kids to ever be given the drug. When summer vacation was over and I was back in school, I had to go to the nurse's office every day at lunchtime so she could give me my pill. That was kind of weird and a little embarrassing sometimes. But it wasn't long before my parents, teachers, and I saw a positive change. My grades skyrocketed; I got almost all A's my seventh grade year, and I didn't even have to study. I was able to sit through an entire class period and not be disruptive. I liked the way I felt, and I loved getting good grades.

But it wasn't meant to last. Since Ritalin had only recently been approved for use by children with A.D.D., the medical community didn't yet know the long-term consequences of kids using the drug. They weren't even sure what the best dosages were. So out of an abundance of caution, my doctors allowed me to take Ritalin for only one year, and then they took me off of it. I definitely felt the loss when I returned to school the following September. I wanted my Ritalin – and my good grades – back!

Now that I'm a grown man with more than four decades behind me, I'm grateful to my doctors and parents for taking me off the drug. I think way too many kids in America were (and still are) being over-medicated and misdiagnosed. Don't get me wrong; I'm not anti-pharmaceutical. I believe in taking medicine when it's necessary. But all children learn differently. I think the education system needs to change to help kids identify their unique characteristics or "flaws" and help them use them in a positive way. Just because a kid is a square peg in a round hole … just because he's a handful at times . . . are no reasons to dope him up for the rest of his life. That's bullshit, and it's tragic because that kid is probably brilliant in his own right, just as he is.

Listen, nobody's perfect. We all have weaknesses. We all have flaws. I believe that for most of us, these defects or weaknesses – when channeled properly and perhaps even celebrated – can become our greatest strengths.

Yes, your flaw may actually be your superpower. That's been my experience. A.D.D. is my superpower, no doubt about it. It gives me an incredible amount of energy, which allows me to multi-task and get a lot of stuff done. My A.D.D. also makes me intense, impulsive, fidgety, anxious, and impatient sometimes. It makes me controlling, scattered, and extremely blunt. But it also helps me get people pumped up and headed in the direction I want them to go. It makes me unafraid of chaos and assertive in the face of conflict. I'm decisive; I take action; I execute. My A.D.D. allows me to be creative at a million miles an hour. Going off on tangents is fun; I love it. Do people think I'm freaking crazy sometimes? Yeah, absolutely. They think I'm a total whack job. But I am a whack job who's fiercely determined to make the most of his superpowers and live a *productive* and happy life. I've never viewed A.D.D. as a negative. Instead, I've embraced it.

Even though I have a potentially *debilitating* "disorder," you shouldn't feel sorry for me. *I've* channeled my A.D.D. onto a positive track and used it to build businesses that have not only made a lot of money but have also made a lot of money for other people and made their lives better. And that's what this book is all about: how my off-the-wall A.D.D. tendencies inspired me to create and execute a set of proven principles for growing a successful business. In the pages that follow, I'll tell you:

- The critical first step toward launching a profitable company

- How to get past the idea stage and actually begin to execute

- A quick technique for keeping your team in lockstep with your vision, every single day

- What I learned about self-promotion from spending eight days with the founder of the Virgin Group, Sir Richard Branson

- My simple "Three Solutions Rule" for solving problems

- Why I recommend acting like a Big Shot, even if you're not one

- How to keep your business moving forward by practicing the Art of Creative Destruction
- The touchy-feely emotion that I believe you must have if you want to grow a profitable company
- How to stop confusing customers and start convincing them to do business with you
- How to channel your psychotic tendencies to create a business and improve your life
- And much more...

I've created numerous profitable companies – including the number one automotive repair chain in North America, a thriving nonprofit youth sports league *and one of the fastest growing franchises in North America* by making the most of my A.D.D. using these principles. I've won numerous awards, grown my net worth to multiple millions, given back to my community, and most importantly, built a great life for myself and my family *and others* using these principles. I believe all that great stuff happened not *despite* my diagnosis, but *because* of it. I didn't conquer A.D.D., I leveraged it! And you can, too.

Look, everybody's got some type of disorder... or two, or four. Find out what yours is, acknowledge it, and use it to help. Don't be ashamed of it. Wear it as a badge of honor. Treat it as an asset, not a deficit. Let it guide you toward living your personal truth. And follow the principles I'm about to outline for you here. They have worked really well for me, and I know they will make a positive difference for you and your business, too.

CHAPTER 1

BEGIN AT
THE BEGINNING

A couple of months ago, my 19-year-old son, Matt Jr., came to me with The Big Question every young adult tackles at some point.

"Dad, what should I do with my life?" he asked. "I know I want to do something *big*. I want to start a business, but I don't know what kind."

"Well, you've got to find something you really like to do," I replied, "and then make a business out of that."

"But how do you find something you really like?"

"You get out there and try a bunch of different stuff. You hang out with people who are smarter than you, and you learn from them."

Matt shook his head, sighed, went into his room and closed the door. Conversation over. And I was okay with that, because I recognized the question, the sigh, and the closed door for what they really were: positive signs that Matt had begun the process of becoming an entrepreneur. I can guide Matt and encourage him as he uncovers his life's purpose, but I can't do the detective work for him. The code is his to crack. This is the first, and arguably the loneliest step, toward achieving success in business — trying a bunch of different things, identifying your strengths, sitting by yourself, searching your soul, and thinking about what you *really* want to do with your life.

IT'S ALL ABOUT THE PASSION

When I was a teenager, I was a lot like Matt, Jr. (and maybe you were too). I knew I wanted to own a business, but I didn't know what kind. From a young age I was fascinated with the business owners I met. Keep in mind that I was a teenager in the 1980s. The culture back then was a lot different from what it is now. Back then not many people were thinking about green living, work/life balance, giving back to the community, or many of the things we are concerned with today. The 1980s were all about me, Me, **ME**. Life was all about materialism, consumerism, and advancing your status. Everybody was watching a new television network called MTV, where we could tune in every day and see how the rock stars lived, who they hung out with, how they dressed, what they drove. The evening television lineup was filled with dramas about glamorous, wealthy families – shows like *Dallas*, *Falcon Crest,* and *Dynasty* dominated the airwaves. Business moguls such as Chrysler's Lee Iacocca and General Electric's Jack Welch were becoming household names. The entrepreneurs I met and saw on television had the high standard of living I wanted. They had money. They had cool houses. They had fast cars… and my friends and I were crazy about cars. Like practically every other kid of my era, I wanted in on that high-status lifestyle, too.

So when I was 15, I went to work in an auto shop in the Washington, D.C. area, near where I lived. I started at the bottom and learned everything there was to know about changing and repairing tires, changing oil, cleaning bathrooms, mopping shop floors. That stuff may not sound appealing to you, but I ate it up with a spoon. I was obsessed. Luckily – thanks to my A.D.D. – I had a ton of energy, which allowed me to spend the time, to put in the hours it took, to become an all-around expert on running a shop without getting burned out or bummed out.

I was also lucky to have had some really good bosses who recognized my passion for cars and helped me channel it in a way that led to profound personal and professional growth. I was promoted into sales and management, where I learned everything about our products and how to sell them. I learned how to manage people effectively, how to provide outstanding customer service, and how to read financial statements. I really dig reading financial statements, which is an essential part of running a successful business. Many people like me with A.D.D. find it difficult to comprehend financial statements because they can't sit still long enough to get a grip on them. But from a young age, I learned to focus my A.D.D. into pinpointing our key indicators and understanding the format of those statements. Now I can buzz right through them in a flash. It's like having enhanced vision and very fast absorption capability... yet another benefit of having A.D.D.!

By the time I was 19, I was making $65,000 a year, and that was in the 1980s. I went on to make millions, all because I followed my heart and went into business doing something I loved... and because I devoted the time and effort it took to become an expert in my field.

YOU'VE GOT TO KNOW YOUR STUFF, MAN.

It's not enough to simply pursue your passion. You have to pursue your passion AND learn everything there is to know about your product or service so you can sell it with confidence. You get that kind of knowledge only by diving in and completely immersing yourself in your chosen industry. Like my dad always said, pick one thing and do it the best you can. I'm a skilled salesman, and I know a lot about tires, parts, operations, marketing, branding, and the automotive business in general. But I don't know anything about computers, so there's no way I would try to start up a computer store.

My point is this: if your passion is information technology and you think you might want to open an IT company someday, go to work for an IT company right now – but not just any random IT company. Go to work for a *great* IT company that has sound policies and procedures in place: a company that makes tons of money, that wins awards for its service and its employee satisfaction. Learn about customer focus from Chick-fil-A… franchising from McDonald's or Chipotle… product development from Apple… employee culture from Virgin or Google. Work for a couple of different companies, and find good mentors at each one.

That's exactly what I did. In the 1980s I went to work as a tire salesman at one of the top Goodyear stores in the country. Back then we would service 50 to 60 cars every day. Customers would bring in their cars in the morning and leave. The technicians would check and diagnose each car. Then the car would sit in the bay while the service manager tried to call the customer back to get the work approved. In those days nobody had cell phones, so sometimes it would take hours to contact the customer. Meanwhile, the car sat there clogging up the bay the entire time. It was an inefficient mess.

But several of the better Goodyear stores came up with a solution: an early morning checkout program. People brought in their cars first thing in the morning. The techs drove them into the bay, checked them, diagnosed them, backed them out of the bay and brought in the next car – checked and diagnosed it, backed it out and brought in the next car, and so on. Nobody actually fixed anything between 7:00 a.m. and 10:00 a.m. All they did was inspect and diagnose cars. By the time a tech got his third car diagnosed, he'd have customer approval and all the parts ready for the first car he'd looked at. From there, the workday flowed like a quart of warm Mobil One. Service was quicker and more efficient. We could fix more cars in one day. Things actually got done. We made more money.

So guess what was the first thing I implemented when I opened my own shop? An early morning checkout program. I would never have known about that killer system had I not done the grunt work at Goodyear.

That's just one example, but there are dozens more. I learned how to talk to customers. I learned how to run a shop efficiently. I learned how to motivate and inspire employees. I learned how to sell tires and auto service. I've sold hundreds of millions of dollars' worth of tires and auto service in the past 32 years. I wouldn't have been that successful had I not learned how to do all the little things in my on-the-job training. I had to wade through a lot of crap to get to those lessons, though...

SEPARATING THE CHAFF FROM THE GRAIN

Speaking of wading through crap, when I was 18 or 19, an employer transferred me to a new store they'd just bought. My job was to re-train the existing store manager on how to run a shop efficiently. The manager was a grumpy old guy who, at ten o'clock every morning, would lurch over to the 7-Eleven across the street to buy a six-pack, which he would stash under the counter. Then his good ol' boy pals would come to the shop with their six-packs, and they'd all sit around and get smashed together. Meanwhile, cars were coming in for oil changes with leaking shocks and bald tires, and nobody was letting the customers know. Nobody was inspecting the cars. The techs were just doing the compulsory oil changes and then shoving all those customers – and all their cash – right out the door because the shop "manager" had better things to do than monitor what was going on and make money for the store. Once I was there to pay attention, we were able to double sales volume at that store within ninety days.

From that experience I learned (a) the value of keeping my head in the game at all times, and (b) how important it is to offer a free inspection and an honest estimate for every car, every visit. I implemented courtesy inspections in all my own shops, and it turned out to be one of our strongest competitive advantages and biggest money makers. I believe – and I taught my people to believe – that it's our job to let our customers know the condition of their vehicles, whether they want to know it or not. That's the way we went to market because that's the way I was taught by all the great shops I worked for when I was younger. I took the good lessons I learned and used them and discarded the bad ones.

This principle applies regardless of the industry you want to get into. Whether passion is guiding you to open an information technology service, a childcare facility, a retail store, a graphic arts studio, an HVAC repair business, or a restaurant, you've got to get to work and learn the ropes first. Countless people have started restaurants because they make great barbecue, yet they "lost their asses" because they had no idea how to run a business. The same goes for automotive technicians starting their own shops. They know how to fix cars, but they tend to be terrible entrepreneurs because they just don't know how to run a business. It's not that they aren't capable of being business leaders. It's just that they never did what it takes to learn business management, and consequently, they fail. I see this happen all the time, and it's sad because it could have been prevented.

I'm a firm believer in making sure you have the core knowledge it takes to outclass the competition. Assembling that knowledge takes time, effort, and energy. Luckily, we A.D.D. entrepreneurs have a leg up on the competition: we have energy to burn. When I was a kid, I was always working. I tried a lot of different things. I sold products door-to-door, cut grass, shoveled driveways, and had a paper route. I began working in the tire and auto industry when I was 15, but I didn't launch my first *really* successful business until I was 28.[1] If that sounds like a long time to wallow around in the trenches, that's because it WAS a long time. But believe me, it was totally worth the investment because it made it easier for me to be successful in the long run.

So, take my advice and begin at the beginning. Identify and pursue your passion. Go out and get some quality experience. Leverage your A.D.D. energy by being willing (and even eager) to start at the bottom and work your ass off. Make your mistakes on somebody else's dime. Be patient, be confident, and be willing to switch gears when necessary. You'll find your right match eventually, and you'll come out on the other side better equipped for entrepreneurial success.

---

1. I had a few successes and failures before that, but that's another book!

GAINING TRACTION #1: A TIP FROM MATT

Life is not about the things you acquire. It's about the people you meet and the experiences you have. It's about the journey. That's why I believe it's so important to travel. Do yourself a huge favor and hit the road every chance you get. I've been all over the world – throughout North, Central, and South America, Australia, Africa, Europe, and Asia – and I have gained so much from it. When you travel, you see life from a whole new perspective, especially if you come from a first-world country and travel to a third- or fourth-world country. You learn a lot and become an all-around happier person. Traveling adds an element of attraction and intrigue to your personality. People gravitate toward those who have *great* stories to tell and experiences to share. This actually empowers you in an indirect way. People are willing to work harder if they see you working your ass off and then bringing back unique experiences that you share. Everyone wins. And you know everyone wants to be on the winning team.

Having adventures is important for your spirit and your soul. I especially love backpacking solo because it gives me time to think and reconnect with myself. It recharges my batteries and helps me be a better husband, dad, neighbor, and entrepreneur. So get out there and see the world. Your life and your business will be better for it.

CHAPTER 2

A.D.D. PIT STOP: WE'RE IN GOOD COMPANY

"Here's to the crazy ones. The misfits. The rebels.
The troublemakers. The round pegs in the square holes.
The ones who see things differently. They're not fond
of rules. And they have no respect for the status quo.
You can quote them, disagree with them, glorify or
vilify them. About the only thing you can't do
is ignore them..."

~ Apple, Inc.

The following is a list of only a few of the athletes, celebrities, and business leaders who have stated publicly that they've been diagnosed with A.D.D./A.D.H.D.[2] You'll notice that there are no slackers here. These folks are living proof that an A.D.D. diagnosis doesn't have to hold you back from achieving your dreams. In fact, most of them have said that A.D.D. was a major contributor to their success. I hope this list inspires you as much as it has me.

Olympic gold medalist: Michael Phelps

Clinton political campaign strategist: James Carville

Jet Blue Airlines founder: David Neeleman

---

2. http://www.addadult.com/add-education-center/famous-people-with-adhd/, accessed August 30, 2014

Dancing with the Stars performer: Karina Smirnoff

Virgin Group founder: Richard Branson

Kinko's founder: Paul Orfalea

Actor and singer: Justin Timberlake

Actor: Jim Carrey

Segway inventor: Dean Kamen

Former quarterback and sports analyst: Terry Bradshaw

TV and radio personality: Glenn Beck

Socialite and businesswoman: Paris Hilton

Emmy-winning actress: Mariette Hartley

Actor and singer: Will Smith

Harvard psychiatrist and
bestselling author: Ed Hallowell, M.D.

Mediabistro CEO: Alan Meckler

Pulitzer Prize-winning writer: Katherine Ellison

…Your Name Goes HERE!

CHAPTER 3

DEVELOP A VISION AND A GAME PLAN

I'm neither a Republican nor a Democrat. I'm a Realist and a Capitalist. Capitalism built America, and I believe it will save America and help the world – which is a core belief of Richard Branson and The Branson School of Entrepreneurship, as well. I believe that capitalism and entrepreneurism can save you and your family, too… but only if you can get past the idea stage and on to the execution stage. Millions of people have great business ideas, but until those ideas are executed, they aren't worth the cocktail napkin they're scribbled on.

This is one thing I know for sure about business: *execution is what separates the entrepreneurs from the "wanna-preneurs."*

So, once you've identified your passion and have racked up some real-world experience in your chosen industry, the next step is to develop your unique vision and a game plan for executing your business idea. You have to know where you're headed (your vision) and how you're going to get there (your game plan). How can you make your company better than the competition? How can you stand out from the rest of the pack? What can you bring to the table that the other guys are missing? What makes you unique, better, different? Figuring that stuff out is the purpose of this step.

If your A.D.D. makes the thought of this kind of intense brainwork a little frightening, don't despair. If I can do it, you can, too. Being easily distracted, having difficulty focusing on things for a long time, and having a hard time paying attention to detail are all very common symptoms for people with A.D.D. I certainly experience all three of these to the maximum level. But these symptoms are not deficits; they are creative superpowers. Take advantage of them! Remember, A.D.D. allows us to multitask and brainstorm better than other people. We can easily work on many projects at once and achieve excellent results. And in my case, I make it a point to surround myself with people who are good at the things I am not good at, and I delegate the details I don't want to do. This gives me more time to focus on developing my vision and my game plan. Ask your associates to carry part of the load so you can devote some time and energy to visioning and planning. More than likely, they'll be very happy to pitch in.

FIND YOUR NICHE AND CREATE
A VISION FOR FILLING IT

Before I went into business for myself, I spent several years working for a couple of auto repair companies that had hundreds of locations. Their size was an advantage in many ways but a disadvantage in others. Most notably, I saw that they were missing out on an entire niche, and a lucrative one at that: the European car market. Owners of high-end cars like BMWs and Porsches weren't patronizing these companies because, quite frankly, they were meat markets. One of them offered a $9.95 oil change, so that ought to tell you everything you need to know about the quality of their service at the time. They didn't have the ability or the wherewithal to attract the area's most qualified technicians; they'd hire anybody who could fog a mirror. They went to market as discounters competing on price, not on quality of service.

On the flip side of the coin were the outstanding small operators I worked for, especially an independent Goodyear store called Craven Tire, which had only four locations. I worked for Craven for years. I'd classify them as more of a boutique shop that didn't try to compete on price. They competed on quality and customer service. They charged more and paid their technicians top dollar, so they did superior work for a higher-end clientele. Craven was a very profitable enterprise with a long-term, sustainable business model.

My vision was to offer what I thought was lacking in the D.C. area: a full-service, high-end, high-quality, trustworthy, custom automotive repair shop with awesome customer service. Because I was already immersed in the industry, I knew exactly how to generate profit using those elements. I had experience running seven different locations for three different companies and had turned every one of those seven locations into the top one or two stores in their respective chains. I doubled, tripled, or quadrupled sales and drove profits to *record levels* in every single store. I figured if I could do it for all those other people, then I could do it for myself.

I did all that by focusing on customer service, being honest, *doing quality work*, and insisting on the same from my technicians and managers. People could only get that level of treatment at a handful of dealerships, and those dealerships were not cheap. Many folks couldn't afford or just didn't want to go there. People want *choices* in the marketplace; they want options. I wanted to be that reasonably-priced alternative but not be the cheapest guy in town. Judy was lock step with this vision and worked tirelessly to build an incredible marketing machine around it.

My goal was to reinvent the automotive repair experience in the D.C. area and to make it better and more accessible than it already was. This is where my obsessive compulsive A.D.D. superpower really helped me. I was obsessed – *literally, clinically obsessed* – with executing my vision. Being obsessive is usually a bad thing, but I used it in a positive way to create a company culture that simply could not be beat. I was determined to offer my customers the options I believed they deserved. I was fanatical about making sure our services were convenient for the customer, not just for us. I wanted to treat them the way I like to be treated when I patronize a business – like family. I decided that my shops would be super clean. We'd have comfortable waiting areas that looked like your family room at home. They'd be stocked with complimentary snacks and hot, fresh coffee. There would be a selection of fun toys for the kids and feminine products in the restrooms for the ladies. I was obsessed with quality. I believed that people wanted to come to an attractive, comfy place to get their cars fixed – a place that did superior quality repairs with great customer service – and I was willing to bet my life on it. As it turns out, I was right.

Ultimately, my employees saw how positively our customers reacted to this crazy, obsessive nature of mine. People kept returning to our shops and bringing their friends and neighbors with them. My employees got excited because they were making more money. The best technicians in town wanted to come to work for us, and I hired them as quickly as I possibly could. Consequently, our workmanship was always of the highest quality. This attracted even *more* customers, even *more* money, even *more* top-notch technicians and managers, and even *more* growth for Curry's Auto Service.

See, I didn't want to play small ball and settle for the status quo in the auto repair industry. I wanted to go big and lay it all on the table. I was so certain of my vision that when I couldn't get a bank loan for my start up, I self-financed it using 13 credit cards.[3]

So that was my vision. What's yours? What's your niche? What makes your product or service unique? How can you use your A.D.D. superpowers to do it better than your competition? Exactly how are you going to pull it off?

That last question is where your game plan comes in.

---

3. I'm not saying that I recommend the credit card route to everyone. I'm only saying that's what I did, and I came out OK. Your mileage may vary.

GAME PLANNING FOR THE A.D.D. ENTREPRENEUR

I am a diehard planner who probably came by the planning gene naturally. I'm the youngest of seven kids in a close knit, gregarious, Irish Catholic family. There are tons of moving parts in a household that size, and I can assure you that nothing got done in my family without some serious advance planning. I've also been involved in team sports my whole life, so I learned early on that being a successful team leader requires preparation. And of course, my A.D.D. requires me to write things down as they occur to me – otherwise my rapid-fire thoughts are gone forever. That's why I'm a staunch advocate for planning things out in advance whenever you can. Other than launching my businesses, I've never been more dedicated to a plan than I was in 2006 when I decided to launch a sports league for the kids in my community.

We live in a planned community with thousands of other families, yet surprisingly, there were no youth sports leagues nearby. Parents had to travel to different counties to get their kids involved in organized athletics. I thought that sucked. I wanted the kids in our neighborhood to have easy access to fun, positive, healthy sports opportunities. So I used my planning and leadership skills to start a nonprofit football league called Dulles South Youth Sports (DSYS). I didn't reinvent the wheel planning DSYS. I simply begged, borrowed, and stole (in a good way!) all the awesome things I saw in other youth sports programs and rolled them into DSYS. It took two years, but it worked. Since its inception, DSYS has expanded beyond football to include cheerleading, wrestling, volleyball, track, cross country, and lacrosse, serving more than 1,600 kids every year. It would have been impossible to get the league off the ground and make it sustainable without sound planning.

Even when I coached a football team of eight-year olds, I made sure we never hit the field without a game plan. By the end of the season, my little elementary school players could perfectly execute 48 different offensive plays. They also had three defensive schemes, as well as special teams plays. That's how determined and well-organized we were. We even recorded the other teams' games and studied the films so we could adjust our plan to fit each competitor. We didn't just go out there and play all willy-nilly with no idea of what was going on. We were serious about developing a game plan and winning. And we had some serious fun.

That's why I'm an advocate of creating a formal game plan for your business. Again, you have to know where you're headed (your vision) and also know how you're going to get there (your game plan). Your plan doesn't have to be in-depth unless you want to make it so, but you do need to write down your vision and an outline of how you intend to execute it, and share it with your stakeholders.

One caveat, though: a game plan is not the same as a business plan. In fact, there's a big debate right now as to whether you should even bother having a traditional business plan. In one camp are the people who think business plans are old school and a total waste of time. In the other camp are those who believe every business must have one, no matter what. I'm in a third camp. I believe some businesses need them but not all. I'm an angel investor who's involved in several companies in addition to my own. I wouldn't even consider investing in a business unless it had both a game plan AND a business plan. If you're seeking funding from outside sources, make a business plan and a game plan. However, if you're financing your venture yourself like I did, you probably won't need a formal business plan. Your time might be better spent focusing on operations and other development that's more vital to your business success. You can always write a business plan later if you want to raise more capital.

But don't slack off when it comes to making your company's game plan. It's the roadmap you and your people will use for making your vision a reality. It's a basic necessity... in football, in business, and in life.

GAINING TRACTION #2: A TIP FROM MATT

Most entrepreneurs like to organize their vision and game plans in some type of visual arrangement, and I'm no exception. That's why I love those big erasable whiteboards. They are a godsend for planners with A.D.D. Writing things down on a big board helps get my thoughts out of my head and into a format my team and I can see. In my meetings I typically have two or three whiteboards stationed around the room so I can record my ideas and my team's input about how we're going to attack whatever it is we're discussing. These days you can even buy electronic whiteboards that print out what you've written on them so you can hand out copies. It's cool technology!

CHAPTER 4

CRAFT A MESSAGE AND SHOUT IT OUT

Once you have a vision and a game plan, it's time to craft your message and share it with the world. If you have a great message and no one knows about it, what good is it? You'll develop two kinds of messages: a big overarching message that explains what your company does and little quick-hit messages that reinforce your main message and keep your people on track.

YOUR MAIN MESSAGE: BEING BLUNT IS A GOOD THING!

To be effective, your main message must be like a good elevator pitch that people can understand in thirty seconds or less. Keep it quick and simple. You don't want to confuse people. You want to convince people, so cut to the chase.

As an example, here's the main message for our original company, Curry's Auto Service:

Quality Care for Your Car – Honest Advice for Our Customer

At Curry's Auto Service, we will:

- Offer our customers honest repair advice about the condition of their vehicles, offer repair options based on need, and ensure that vehicles are repaired properly and professionally the first time, with high quality parts.

- Treat our customers and their cars with the highest regard and offer superior customer relations, keep open lines of communication with our customers to ensure that their cars are diagnosed and repaired correctly and efficiently, and address any and all customer concerns.

- Provide a clean environment for both our customers and their cars.
- Exceed our customers' expectations in every way.

And here's the main message for our new company, **The Hybrid Shop**.

The Hybrid Shop will:

- Build an international dealer network of professional auto repair shops who are knowledge leaders in the diagnosis, service, repair, and maintenance of hybrid vehicles using proven scientific methods.
- Increase our dealers' revenue streams by providing value-added services, diagnostics, and repairs, enabling our dealers to surpass the expectations of hybrid owners and meet the new demands of the growing hybrid and electric vehicle aftermarket repair industry within their communities while increasing their profits.

Once you have your main message hammered out, you'll need to begin spreading the gospel to your people, your community, and your current and potential customers. You can't just declare your message one time and expect it to stick. You have to say it every chance you get, over and over, consistently... obsessively. Enforce and reinforce that message, and keep following up until carrying out the message becomes second nature for your whole team.

TWO-MINUTE MEETINGS KEEP YOU AND YOUR PEOPLE FOCUSED

At Curry's Auto Service, I insisted that all of our managers conduct brief meetings throughout the day to keep our main message front and center in everyone's minds. This is where the little quick-hit "drive-by" messages I mentioned earlier come into play. We'd usually have a lull in the action sometime between 9:00 a.m. and 10:00 a.m. each day and occasionally another one mid-afternoon. During those slower moments, I'd have the managers get everybody together for what we called a "two-minute meeting" and say something like, "Hey, we're really busy today guys, so keep your heads in the game. Make sure you inspect every single car and test drive each one before and after service. Double check everything. Remember, it's all about quality, so do your best work. Keep the shop clean, and use seat covers and floor mats in every car."

The following day, the two-minute meeting message might be, "Hey, we're not very busy today guys, so keep your heads in the game. It's really important that you test drive and inspect every car because we don't have very many coming in today. Remember, it's all about quality, so do your best work. Keep the shop clean, and use seat covers and floor mats in every car."

You see, the message was the same no matter whether we were busy or slow. Every word out of my and my managers' mouths was designed to circle back and underscore the company's main message. This is an effective technique not only for A.D.D. business owners and managers to keep themselves on track but also to re-establish the focus of any employees who might have A.D.D.

Here's another way I used two-minute meetings to reinforce our core message. We embraced technology early on at Curry's Auto Service, but it wasn't always easy getting everyone on board. When we opened our first shop in March of 1998, the Internet was just emerging as a useful business tool. Not many people were online yet. Still, we recognized the potential of the Internet and email to help us build our business. Our marketing budget was pretty lean, but we knew that if we could connect with customers through email, we could market to them for free. We could sign them up for a useful and relevant electronic newsletter and send them reminders about oil changes and other services they might need, which would be much cheaper than sending out mailings through the post office. Most importantly, we could continually reinforce and control our message and stay top of mind when auto repair came up. If we were top of mind, our customers would be more apt to share us with their friends, families, and co-workers. Best ROI ever!

We launched our first website and started using email immediately after opening the store in 1998. For the first eight months, not much happened for us online. But as we all know, the Internet caught on, and more people started communicating via email. We ramped up our efforts to add email addresses to our data collection, but it wasn't working. My employees had no problem asking customers for their name, address, and telephone number, but they were not used to or comfortable asking for email addresses. You wouldn't believe all the excuses my people gave for not getting them. The most common reason was that customers just didn't want to give out their email address because they didn't want more messages in their inbox. But the reality was that 95% of customers gave them when asked.

Training my team to ask for emails was a real "pain-in-the-ass" but we stuck with it because we knew it had the potential to make or break our business. We would literally go through 300 to 400 tickets every day to see which employees were collecting email addresses and which ones weren't. I had countless two-minute meetings in which I reminded everybody to get the email addresses and explained why doing so would lead to more business, which would lead to more income and job security for them. It took three years of concentrated effort, but eventually my team caught on and we got to almost 100% compliance.

This was a huge achievement for us, because it made it easy for us to communicate with our customers frequently and efficiently. We sent thousands of monthly email reminders, which kept us top of mind with our customers. This not only drove traffic to our stores, but it also significantly reduced our marketing costs and added value to our company. By the time we sold Curry's Auto Service in 2013, we had over 100,000 email addresses and over

28,000 people opted in on our monthly electronic newsletter. I credit yet another of my A.D.D. superpowers – my power of intuition – for helping me recognize and seize the marketing opportunity provided by early Internet technology.

BE OBSESSIVE: ENFORCE, REINFORCE, AND REFINE THE MESSAGE – INTERNALLY AND EXTERNALLY

Your business is going to move forward. Your game plan is dynamic, not static. When new policies, procedures, and technologies are implemented, you can't just deliver the message once and expect people's behaviors to change in an instant. You've got to go back and continually preach that message. You've got to enforce it and reinforce it, like we did with acquiring the email addresses.

That's how messaging (or what I call internal marketing) works within your company. But how about getting your core message out the door to the masses? You must never let a good marketing opportunity go to waste. When you make a good hire, let the world know about it. Press release the hell out of everything.[4] You want to constantly be talking about yourself and your company and looking for creative ways to deliver the word.

Networking is one way. Seek out fun networking events, but make sure you're not wasting your time rubbing elbows with people who bring nothing to the table. Networking means developing value-added relationships, not just drinking martinis and passing business cards around.

I'm in a couple of groups that have added *awesome* value to my life, both personally and professionally. First of all, I'm a member of Maverick1000, a private, invitation-only group of international entrepreneurs. Founded by digital marketing expert and bestselling author Yanik Silver, Maverick1000 brings

---

4. Within reason, of course. Don't put out press releases about stupid things. Make sure they're about something newsworthy. Get help from a good public relations or marketing professional if you're not confident you can handle it on your own. It will be money well spent.

its members together numerous times every year for retreats where we have access to continuing education, get to hear informative speakers, and participate in leadership exercises, adventure travel, and philanthropy. We've hung out with kickass entrepreneurs and inspiring leaders like Zappos CEO Tony Hsieh, Hip Hop legend Russell Simmons, Tony Hawk, Jesse James, Super Bowl Champ Carl Banks, X-Prize creator Dr. Peter Diamandis, and Richard Branson. The Maverick motto is *Have More Fun, Make More Money, Give More Back*. We have a mission in Haiti that we travel to and support. We've mentored budding entrepreneurs worldwide. It's extremely rewarding and always a great adventure.

Maverick has become more than just a networking and educational opportunity for me. It's like a fraternity really, because there are hundreds of Mavericks all over the world I can call upon to give me advice and support – and even a place to crash if I need one. They all know they can count on me for the same, too. I've made some really great lifelong friends and connections through Maverick. I recommend that every aspiring business leader read Yanik's excellent book, *34 Rules for Maverick Entrepreneurs: More Profits, More Fun & More Impact*.[5]

Another networking group that I've found to be worthwhile is Cadre DC, which was created by leading financial advisor Derek Coburn and his wife, Melanie. Derek is the bestselling author of *Networking is Not Working: Stop Collecting Business Cards and Start Making Meaningful Connections*[6] (which is also on my recommended reading list, by the way). Cadre is a connector network of the top entrepreneurs and business owners in the Washington DC, Maryland, and Virginia areas. Like Maverick, it is an exclusive group designed to help its members develop long-term, meaningful, valuable relationships – not just

---

5. http://www.amazon.com/34-Rules-Maverick-Entrepreneurs-Profits-ebook/dp/B00JPJQ2UY/ ref=la_B002BM64UA_1_4?s=books&ie=UTF8&qid=1407697876&sr=1-4 accessed August 10, 2014.

6. http://www.amazon.com/Networking-Not-Working-Collecting-Connections-ebook/dp/ B00K436RH8/ref=tmm_kin_swatch_0?_encoding=UTF8&sr=1-1&qid=1407698064 accessed August 10, 2014

superficial, empty connections. Both Maverick and Cadre make it possible for me to hang out with people who are way smarter than me and who have helped me grow as a person and a leader. Do yourself a favor and find similar groups in your area. Don't just go to the standard Chamber of Commerce events that are attended by anybody and everybody. Stretch yourself. Being a part of high caliber networking groups will not only help you get your message out but also will help you polish and refine that message until it sparkles.

Another way to spread the word is by doing cool stuff in your community. One of our goals with Curry's Auto Service was to *"Serve the Communities We Service,"* so we gave our time, money, energy, and resources to every town in which we operated. For example, my wife, Judy, once organized a 5K run to benefit DSYS. Over 300 runners participated, and we got lots of press coverage. We also gave $15,000 to the DSYS program and were featured on the front pages of a bunch of community newspapers. We sponsored all the local car clubs and hosted open houses for them at our shops. We also went to their gatherings and contributed raffle prizes for their events. We would race and instruct at their drivers' education days and advertise in their magazines. By doing all that, we gained the car club members' trust, and they rewarded us with their business.

But that's not all we did. We hired local artists to paint incredible murals on the ugly exterior walls of several of our buildings. We were involved in homeless shelters and soup kitchens. We held car clinics for women. We sponsored teen driving clinics. We opened our shops for Girl Scouts and Boy Scouts who were trying to earn their automotive badges. We did something community-minded in every store as often as we possibly could. All that helped us build our presence and kept us top of mind.

It's the same idea as building name recognition for a political candidate. People tend to vote for the person whose name they recognize, even if they don't have the slightest idea what that person stands for. You have to market yourself and put your name and your message out there so potential customers will see it and remember you.

One person who knows how to fully seize marketing opportunities is Sir Richard Branson, founder of the Virgin Group. Although we'd already done a lot of successful marketing at Curry's Auto Service before I met Richard, getting to know him really hammered home the concept of self-promotion for me. I've been fortunate to go on safari with him and also spent eight days with him on his private island. He's done a lot of crazy stunts in the name of promoting his companies: driving an amphibious car across the English Channel; trying to sail a hot air balloon around the world; shaving off his beard, putting on a $10,000 wedding dress, and walking a catwalk in front of the paparazzi; bungee jumping off the top of a Las Vegas hotel . . . all in the name of promoting his companies. With a net worth of around $5 billion, I'd say Richard's escapades have worked out pretty well for him.

I haven't gone as far as Branson has to generate buzz, but I've had some fun adventures of my own. I flew a Russian MIG-29 fighter jet up to 77,000 feet and saw the curvature of the earth and outer space, then came back and did aerobatics at 4,000 meters, finishing with an inverted fly-over 15 meters above the airstrip. I've backpacked through Central America and Asia. I spent a week with the Hill Tribe village people near the Burma border. I've hiked the Inca Trail to Machu Picchu. I dove with great white sharks in Shark Alley in South Africa. I went on safari with Richard at his private reserve in Ulusaba, South Africa and spent eight days on his private retreat, Necker Island.

I didn't always tell people about my private life and all the things I was doing because I didn't want to brag or have my employees or customers be jealous. But thanks to Branson's influence, I'm now letting everybody know about my adventures. It's been amazing. Wherever I go people come up to me and want to talk about what I've been doing lately. Then they tell others, which generates more interest. When people become interested in me, they also become interested in my newest venture, **The Hybrid Shop**.

And that's what shameless self-promotion is all about. I believe wholeheartedly in the core messages I created for my companies. I want the whole wide world to know about them. Anything positive I can do to spread the word, I'm on it. So develop a compelling message, and then seek out creative ways to deliver it everywhere you go. Say it loud, say it proud, and say it *often*. Shout it out!

GAINING TRACTION #3: A TIP FROM MATT

How many times have you seen this happen? You have a meeting with your managers to pass on important information that you want disseminated throughout the ranks. You tell the managers your message; they nod and walk out of the meeting... and nothing happens. Your information either doesn't get passed along because the managers got busy with something else, or it gets passed along but important stuff is lost in the translation. That doesn't do anybody a damn bit of good. *That's why I insist that my managers have a two-minute meeting with their people immediately after leaving my office or ending our conference call.* That way the information we just discussed is still fresh in their minds when they relay it to their team, and I can go on with my day feeling confident that my message got out. I even insist on two-minute meetings when there is no new news, just so I can enforce/re-enforce my primary corporate message.

CHAPTER 5

OVERCOME CHALLENGES

One of the greatest thrills and loves of my life is car racing. I've been doing it since the 1980s. I've raced at Silverstone Raceway in England, Canada's Mont-Tremblant, and all along the east coast of the United States. For a long time I even instructed other people on how to race. The most important thing I learned and taught my racing students was the necessity of looking ahead. When you're flying around a race track at 150 miles per hour, you can't just peer down the nose of the car and expect to live long. You've got to look far into the future, as far as your eyes can see around the next couple of turns, so you'll have sufficient time to react to whatever opportunities or obstacles are coming up.

This concept of looking ahead and predicting the future has applications beyond racing. Before you can solve any problem – whether it's in your business, on the race track, or in your personal life – you have to see it first. The sooner you recognize it, the better the odds you'll be able to take corrective action to fix it before too much damage is done. This is really important. The best entrepreneurs can see around corners and look over mountains. They're always peering into the future and analyzing what they see. Clairvoyance is an awesome superpower, but clarity – recognizing the real problem – is key. Like I always say, I'm not a *salesman*; I'm a hyperactive *problem solver*.

Many of us with A.D.D. are extremely hyperactive. This hyperactivity is not just the outward physical kind; it's also mental. For me, my hyperactivity "disorder" enables my probability superpower to predict outcomes in advance. The ability to understand a problem at its core, quickly come up with a solution, and take action are important qualities for any leader. By being able to forecast the outcome in advance, my A.D.D. helps me solve problems, speak bluntly, and execute swiftly.

THE THREE-SOLUTIONS RULE

Once you recognize that there is a problem brewing, I advocate coming up with three possible solutions. This is the strategy I teach to all my employees, and it's made a huge, positive difference in my businesses. Here's an example of how it works. Let's say my tech (who's looking ahead and seeing around corners like he's been trained to do) realizes that a customer's car is not going to be ready on time because the wrong part came in, and that customer has to pick up her son from daycare in a couple of hours. He notifies the manager. The manager (who's also been trained to stay on top of the wave) begins brainstorming three workable solutions to this dilemma. Getting the car fixed on time is not possible, so that's not one of the solutions. He decides that he could give the client a ride to pick up her son. That's one solution. He could get her a rental car even if he has to go to the airport to find one. That's another solution. Or he could loan her his own car or a company car. That's solution number three. Once the manager has come up with three solutions, he'll meet with the customer and empower her by letting her choose the one that makes the most sense to her. By the time she and her child get back to the shop, the right part will have come in, and the car will be ready to go.

When considering which route to take, don't overcomplicate things and become paralyzed. Just figure out what the *real* problem is, and fix it. In the above example, the problem is not that the car isn't going to be ready on time – that's just static in the background. The real problem is that the customer has to pick up her son from daycare soon and will not have a way to get there. That's the actual, immediate issue that needs to be resolved.

It's all about dealing with reality and keeping things simple. Don't jump to conclusions and create unnecessary drama. Just break the thing down, come up with three solutions, pick one, and move on. One of the blessings of having A.D.D. is that it is relatively easy for us to come up with different ways to overcome an obstacle and then make a quick pivot if it doesn't work out. Like I always told my guys, it's OK if you make a decision and it turns out to be wrong. At least you made a decision, which is more than many people do. Regroup and make another run at solving the problem.

THE A.D.D. ENTREPRENEUR ALWAYS FINDS A WAY... OR MAKES ONE!

I learned about problem solving the hard way. Like I said in a previous chapter, I started my business with $103,000 on 13 credit cards, a $200,000 equipment loan that I had no idea how I was going to repay, and a $35,000 loan from my father-in-law (what's scarier than that?). My first location was in the back of a terrible little industrial park far away from any main roads. It was super hard to find, yet we were busy from the moment we opened the doors. I'd lived in that area my entire life, and I'd already been working in the automotive business for a long time, so I had built up a following of loyal fans. Also, I'd advertised by putting fliers on the windshields of cars and some of the other improvised stuff you do when you have no marketing budget. And by the grace of God, we generated sales right away. We did $800,000 in sales our first nine months in business and $1.6 million our first full year. So what's this got to do with problem solving?

Well, the problem was that I ran out of parking spots. My product was cars, yet I had no place to park them because my location had only four parking spaces. Even the least popular auto shop in the world would find that problematic. So I quickly expanded and bought an adjacent building, which gave me a grand total of seven parking spots. Keep in mind that my shop was in a crowded industrial park. There was an air-conditioning company next door that had 30 trucks parked all over the place. We were friendly with them, but still, we used to get into it from time to time because we were all jockeying for space. It was a nightmare.

But behind our building was another industrial complex, and it had a big unused parking lot. The only thing separating me from that empty lot was a tree line. You could literally walk ten feet from my shop through the tree line and into that vacant parking lot, but by car it was a mile's drive. I used to stand back there shaking my head and thinking, "Damn! If only I had that lot!" It was torturous… so close, but yet so far. One day I just couldn't take it anymore and started parking cars back there. I didn't seek the owner's consent. I decided I'd rather beg for forgiveness than ask for permission. I'm not very good with rules.

Eventually – six months later, to be exact – the parking lot's owner caught on and ordered me to cease and desist from parking cars on his property. So I made a deal with him: I'd rent 15 of his parking spaces for $500 a month. He said OK, but it's a cash-only deal. I'd have to personally go in and pay him the first of every month. I said fine, *whatever it takes*. I had to do what I had to do. I needed the parking spaces.

The only wrinkle was that this dude had an enormous, snarling Doberman Pinscher and a "big ass" growling Rottweiler sitting just inside his door at all times. He never even tried to control those dogs: never ordered them to heel or told them to shut up or anything. He just let them do whatever they felt like doing. Whenever I came in to make my monthly payment, I would have to run the gauntlet between those two horrible dogs nipping at my heels. I'd take a deep breath, dash in, throw the $500 down on the desk, and dash out before I got eaten by the Rottweiler and the Doberman. It was terrifying. But I got to keep my parking spaces, which allowed my business to prosper and grow.

That's what it takes to overcome challenges sometimes. You suck it up and do what you have to do to solve the problem.

RALLYING THE TROOPS

And if you don't know what to do to solve the problem, phone a friend. When you have A.D.D., things fall through the cracks sometimes. But if you surround yourself with people whose own superpowers fill in the gaps for you, that's when you strike gold. That's the way it's been for me with my wife, Judy. We've accomplished a lot together. One of her superpowers is attention to detail, which is something I lack. Teaming up with Judy was the smartest thing I've ever done, because I know there's no way in hell I could have made it this far without her.

Another of the best things I've ever done for myself personally and professionally was to join a Twenty Group, which is a group of (you guessed it) 20 other automotive repair shop owners and entrepreneurs. We would get together three times a year and talk about ideas, best practices, financials, problems, and opportunities. Then we'd come up with action items and hold each other accountable. Many people in the group have become great friends over the years. We've had a lot of fun together, but more importantly, I have learned a tremendous amount from them. Whenever I was stumped by a problem, I knew I could call one or more members of my Twenty Group for excellent advice. Your chosen industry likely has similar groups and associations you can join. Use these groups to create a network of trusted advisors and experts you can call upon in a pinch.

Another smart thing I did was hire a great business coach by the name of Jody Ruth. I worked with Jody for two years, and it was some of the best time and money I've ever spent because she helped me fill in the gaps in my skill set and helped me expand my point of view. You see, I never earned a college degree. After high school graduation, I went to college full time and worked part time; then I switched to going to school part time and working full time. You might recall that I was already earning $65,000 a year by the time I was nineteen years old, and that was in the 1980s. Back then people were graduating with law degrees and only making $30,000 a year. Eventually I got to a point in my career where I had to make a decision about the direction I was going to take. I ended up dropping out of college because I didn't feel like education was important to me, but I had a change of heart later in my career when I met Jody.

Jody is a CPA and a CGMA (chartered global management accountant). For over thirty years she has worked in a variety of industries in high-stakes positions. She has served as a senior finance and operations leader at a Fortune 50 corporation, a senior audit and consulting lead for key clients for a Big Four accounting firm, and as an outsourced CFO to growth firms across technology, telecom, satellite, mobile, online, government contracting, transportation, and various other industries. She's an expert at corporate strategy, especially when it comes to growth, scaling, and exiting.

Because of her education and high-level experience, Jody has a completely different way of thinking than I do. Her way of thinking isn't better or worse than mine – only different. Working with her was good for me; we got along really well. She helped me plan my company's growth strategy and helped me capitalize on my personal strengths and A.D.D. superpowers. She also helped me realize that there are many different ways to get an education. College is one of those ways, but so are learning on the job and learning by surrounding yourself with smart people. Jody was an awesome partner and sounding board. With her help I gained the confidence to make changes to my business that I might not otherwise have had the insight or the courage to make – changes that paid off substantially for me later on down the line. I highly recommend investing in someone like Jody to help you become a better business leader.

Being an entrepreneur can be lonely, but you don't have to go it alone. Build a network of really smart, trusted advisors who will help you overcome your challenges. Don't hang out with people who have nothing to bring to the table. Use your A.D.D. superpowers to learn to see around corners. Be proactive. Don't overthink. Focus on the solution, not the problem. And don't be afraid to face the big dogs in the hallway. Trust me – in most cases their bark is much worse than their bite.

GAINING TRACTION #4: A TIP FROM MATT

Peer groups and coaching are great, but proceed with caution. First of all, ensure that linking up with a group or coach will be worthwhile and relevant to your goals. If a person or group has nothing to offer you personally or professionally, just say no. Second, don't overcommit. At one time I was in five different groups and had so much going on that I didn't have time for my business anymore. I had to let a couple of things go. Don't get so caught up in networking that you neglect your work. Your company has to be your number one focus. Sometimes it even has to come before your family. When I started my company, I basically kissed my wife, Judy, and said, "Bye, honey. I'll see you in a couple of years." That's the way it works. If you're going to be in business, you've got to **be in business**. Period!

CHAPTER 6

A.D.D. PIT STOP: MIRROR TRAITS

*"Change the way you look at things,
and the things you look at change."*

~ Dr. Wayne Dyer

I believe that words have energy – tangible, palpable energy. Consequently, the words we use to describe ourselves have a profound effect on our self-esteem and our actions. When we pick negative words to describe our A.D.D., we cut ourselves down and diminish our abilities. But whenever we choose to put a positive spin on our condition, we lift ourselves up and come away empowered.

The following table is from The Hallowell Center, an organization that specializes in the diagnosis and treatment of A.D.D.[7] I'm not associated with The Hallowell Center, but I really like this comparison of negative and positive ways to label common A.D.D. traits. If you usually describe yourself using words from the left side of the chart, try substituting the accompanying positive words from the right side of the chart, and see if it changes your attitude about your condition and your capabilities.

---

7. http://www.hallowellnyc.com/HallowellNYC/LivingwithADD/
   BenefitsYesBenefitsofHavingADDA/index.cfm, accessed August 31, 2014.

Negative A.D.D. Associated Trait	Accompanying, Positive Trait
Distractible	Curious
Impulsive	Creative
Hyperactive, Restless	Energetic
Intrusive	Eager
Can't stay on point	Sees connections others miss
Forgetful	Totally involved in what he/she is doing
Disorganized	Spontaneous
Stubborn	Persistent, won't give up
Inconsistent	Shows flashes of brilliance
Moody	Sensitive

CHAPTER 7

THINK BIG
AND EXECUTE

Thanks to my A.D.D., no matter what I'm doing – whether I'm working or playing – I'm going big. When I throw a party, I throw a **PARTY**. When I create a nonprofit youth sports league, I create a **NONPROFIT YOUTH SPORTS LEAGUE**. When I start a business, I start a **BUSINESS**. I believe in going big or going home. All the best entrepreneurs I've ever met are the same way. To me, this is the mark of a great business leader. A lot of "wanna-preneurs" kind of stick their big toe in the water and mumble, "Okay, I guess I'm sort of in business now…" but they're not *really* in business. To win at this game of commerce and capitalism, you've got to execute. You've got to put everything on the line. No holds barred. No Plan B.

THE LAND, AIR, AND SEA APPROACH

When we started **The Hybrid Shop**, we went all in and spent over $400,000 on marketing in our first eight months. We weren't content to just let the folks in our immediate area know what we were doing. We wanted to tell the whole wide world. So we took what I call a Land, Air, and Sea approach to publicizing our launch. We spread the word about our new venture using every means available to us. We press released it. We built a kick-ass website: Internet, SEO, pay-per-click, newspaper, radio… we used every one, early and often. We even hired the legendary quarterback Terry Bradshaw to do a five-minute educational video that went nationwide on the Discovery Channel in 36 targeted markets. Our goal was to get the masses excited about **The Hybrid Shop**.

If you don't have hundreds of thousands of dollars to spend on marketing, don't despair. There are plenty of ways to go big on a budget. Use social media to your advantage. Become a media darling. Develop relationships with local business journalists, and get them to write about you, and then ask them for introductions to their friends at larger publications. Reporters are busy people. Make their lives easier by letting them know they can come to you whenever they need a source for a story. Reporters need quick access to experts they can call upon for interviews when their deadline is crashing down around them. Let one of those experts be you. Everybody wins. The journalist gets a good story, and you get positive publicity.

Don't be afraid to leverage your existing relationships. Most people will be eager to assist you, so ask for what you want. Build a team of advocates and cheerleaders who will help you spread the word. That's how I got some of my biggest breaks early on. For example, the president of the local BMW club once came in for service, and he was so happy afterward that he wrote an awesome article about us in the local BMW Club magazine. That brought instant credibility to Curry's Auto Service. Soon we had BMWs piling into our stores, all thanks to that one vocal cheerleader. Also, one of our neighbors was a television executive. I told him about my new shop and he got me a really good deal on airtime for a commercial. I could only afford that one commercial, so I made it the best it could be.

Even if you can only afford one 15-second radio spot, do it. Then put it on your website so everyone knows you're on the radio. The trick is to always act and look bigger than you are. Back when I had one little store, I acted as if I had ten of the most profitable stores in America. People want to deal with a bigger company – or at least they want to *think* they're dealing with a bigger company. Size (even if it's only perceived size!) matters. It lends an air of legitimacy to your business.

So execute your game plan with confidence, as if you're already an industry leader... but don't let your plan get in the way of your forward motion. Your business is not going to look the same tomorrow as it does today. It's going to evolve and grow. Don't be rigid. Be nimble. That's the beauty of having A.D.D. and running a small-ish business. You have the freedom and the ability to turn on a dime whenever the situation calls for it. If something's not working or if a new opportunity arises, you can – you must – adjust.

THE A.D.D. ENTREPRENEUR'S FAVORITE PASTIME: CREATIVE DESTRUCTION

Even when things are going really well, you must continue to fine-tune your systems, services, and products. This is what I call "practicing creative destruction." Like most people with A.D.D., I am rarely happy with the status quo. I don't like to wait in line, and I hate to wait my turn. I'm restless, impatient, anxious, and seldom satisfied. I use these "flaws" as my creative destruction superpowers and aim them toward always trying to improve our product or service. Sure, my impatience causes me to miss things sometimes. But at least I'm not spending my life waiting in line!

When I owned Curry's Auto Service, we were voted the #1 Auto Repair Shop in North America by *Motor Age* magazine. We had a good thing going. We had great people and sound policies and procedures. Our folks did things the right way. They test drove every vehicle before and after they worked on it. They inspected every car without fail, and they gave superior customer service. Still, I wasn't satisfied. I was always trying to break things down and see how we could make our company better and more efficient.

For example, we had really nice showrooms in our first four stores. They were always clean, neat, and pleasant. But when we were preparing to open our fifth store, my wife, Judy, decided that the status quo wasn't good enough for our new location. So we put down hardwood floors and furnished our new showroom with high-end leather couches and flat screen TVs. Judy and I liked the way it looked so much that we ended up spending a couple hundred thousand dollars to refurbish all of our showrooms the same way. We never thought, "Cool! Things are just fine around here. Let's go to the beach." No. We were always looking for ways to improve our showrooms, our policies, our procedures, our website, our company culture, our customer service, our social media approach. We were determined to keep moving forward, and we continue to practice creative destruction with our newest venture, **The Hybrid Shop**. We're always looking for ways to improve.

LEVERAGE YOUR RELATIONSHIPS WITH YOUR CUSTOMERS AND YOUR TEAM

One of the best ways to keep moving forward is to listen to your customers. We once had an outside company come in and conduct a qualitative survey in which they interviewed about 40 of our customers for as long as they could keep them on the phone. We wanted to find out exactly what our customers wanted from us. Wow, did they ever tell us! We ended up making some beneficial changes as a result of that survey. Be careful, though. When you ask your customers what they want, you have to be prepared to give it to them. I mean, you *really* have to be prepared to set your ego aside, hit the reset button, and make adjustments to your execution. Otherwise, what's the point in asking for customer feedback?

To execute your game plan properly, you not only have to listen to your patrons but also practice the best and highest use of your company's human capital. You have to figure out what you and each member of your team excels in, and then put everybody on the task they're built for and let them do their thing. My best and highest use is not sitting in the office reading a 47-page contract. Details make me crazy. Thanks to my ability to see the big picture (yet another of my A.D.D. superpowers!) my best and highest use is in strategy and operations. It's in the game planning, visioning, and in getting people pumped up about executing the plan.

Having said that, you need to be willing and able to do anything when you're an entrepreneur, especially when you're first starting out. When I launched Curry's Auto Service, I dealt with all the customers, billed people in and out, changed oil, changed tires, cleaned bathrooms, and mopped floors. That was my best and highest use at the time. Right now that would not be the case.

Again, it all comes down to making beneficial adjustments as you go along. As your business evolves, people's roles will change. Your job is to be aware: to get to know your team members and understand their interests and capabilities so you can put everyone into the right seat on the bus. Sometimes a person's best and highest use doesn't reveal itself for a while. My sister, Susan, is a *perfect* example of that. Susan is our accountant. She has a degree in accounting and is a detail-oriented numbers person. But as it turns out, she's also super creative. Susan absolutely loves planning our parties and events, and she's great at it. Who knew? She's my oldest sister and has worked with us for ten years, yet I didn't know about that awesome aspect of her personality and that terrific skill set until recently. I'm so glad Susan's event planning abilities were exposed so we could begin utilizing her in that capacity, because we've all benefited so much from it.

BE A SMOOTH OPERATOR BY LEVERAGING YOUR HEIGHTENED AWARENESS

Like I said before, when it comes to executing your business operations, your job is to **be aware**. In order to be aware, you must have boots on the ground so you can personally survey your kingdom and take the pulse of your business. You've got to be physically, mentally, and emotionally present – constantly interacting with your team and talking with your customers – if you want your business to operate according to your vision.

I once had an operations guy who came to us with a lot of experience as a regional manager. I'll call him Ted. We liked Ted's resume, and he talked a good game. *So we hired him as a Store Manager and then promoted him to Operations Manager* for eleven different locations, including the corporate office, and to oversee more than 150 employees who were serving around 5,000 customers a month. After a few months on the job, it became clear that something was wrong. Too many critical things were falling through the cracks; too many problems were cropping up and getting worse rather than being resolved.

I defended Ted. I thought he was trying really hard and simply needed time to adjust to all the moving parts in our business. So I gave him more time, and I tried everything I could think of to help him succeed. Nothing seemed to work. I *continued* to defend Ted and give him the benefit of the doubt, but eventually I had to admit that the situation just wasn't getting better. So I put out an email survey in which I asked my employees what they thought of Ted's management style. I didn't hire an outside company to do the survey; I created it myself in about five minutes and sent it out on a whim (yet another example of my A.D.D. kicking into full gear). I was stunned when the responses came back. It was like an avalanche of shitty news. It turns out that there was zero respect for Ted among the employees. He wasn't motivating the staff. In fact, they hardly ever saw him. I had no idea where Ted was all day, but he wasn't in my stores. The salary I was paying him was basically being tossed out the window. So I fired him. I would never have known the truth had I not faced the issue head on and asked my people for their feedback.

Generally speaking, if something's not going right in a business, it's because there has been a breakdown in the vision and/or the game plan. You've got to figure out where that breakdown is. In order to do that, you've got to step into the chaos. You've got to physically be there to examine your operations. Again, this is where having A.D.D. can be a real benefit for entrepreneurs. People with A.D.D. do not fear chaos; we embrace it. We can jump into the middle of the mayhem and quickly establish order and control. We can focus through the static to bring clarity and clearness to any situation. This enables us to find alternate paths to overcome obstacles and to be able to take on large issues and get a grip on them.

In my case, my A.D.D. and obsessive-compulsive tendencies often save the day. Although A.D.D. symptoms vary from person to person, obsessive-compulsive "disorder" is certainly closely associated and related to A.D.D. I use my obsessive-compulsive superpower in a positive way to be obsessive over the things I can control and improve in my personal life and in my business.

For example, whenever I had a store that was underperforming, I'd stop whatever I was doing and focus like a laser on finding the reason why. I'd go through every single scrap of related paperwork, and I could usually tell pretty quickly why sales weren't up to par. Maybe the technicians weren't inspecting cars properly, or the sales people weren't saying yes on the phone often enough, or they weren't presenting as many estimates as normal. Had I been off doing other things, I would not have been able to focus on solving the problem, and I might have (a) not been able to fix the breakdown until it was too late, or (b) completely missed the fact that there was a breakdown in the first place.

The bottom line is that whether you have A.D.D. or not, you cannot try to rule your world by email. Back when I had only a few stores, I used to visit each of them twice a week. But as our business expanded, it became impossible for me to keep up that pace. I needed help. I had a business partner who served as my operations guy. He was a terrific person. But as the years went by, he didn't want to work as many hours as he had before. His kids were getting to the age where they were involved in sports, and he wanted to be a big part of that. I'm into sports and I have kids too, so I understood his position. However, he started taking off early most days so he could make it to his kids' practices and games on time, and without him around to stay on top of things, the business began to suffer.

You (or your trustworthy, committed designee) MUST be involved and executing your vision and game plan on a day-to-day basis. You simply cannot be an absent owner and expect your business to last for very long. This is one of those times when you have to be present to win!

To recap, it does you no good to have a vision and a plan unless you execute them. Think big. Take a Land, Air, and Sea approach to your marketing. Be a media darling; never let a promotional opportunity go to waste. Have a plan, but don't let it get in the way of your progress. Give your A.D.D. energy and impatience full rein, and use them to keep moving forward and improving by practicing creative destruction. Implement the best and highest use of your company's human capital, but be willing to do anything. Be fully present and manage by walking around. And remember: perception is reality, so act as if you're already an industry leader. The customers, the accolades, and the profits will follow.

GAINING TRACTION #5: A TIP FROM MATT

One of the quickest, most reliable ways to determine the best and highest use of your company's human capital is to have your key employees take personality tests. These tests reveal not only how people tend to think but also how they tend to behave... how readily they accept criticism, how well they listen, how willing they are to admit mistakes, how eager they are to collaborate, how gracefully they handle pressure or conflict.

You can have these tests administered to yourself and your existing team members, and/or make personality testing part of your hiring process. Test the top performers on your team – the people you really like and who best fit in with your company's culture – so you can identify their personality profiles and most appealing traits. Then use that information to hire others who possess similar attributes. Keep in mind, however, that the characteristics that make up a great CFO are not necessarily the ones that make up the best salesperson or technician. Each of those positions requires a different personality type. So if you're looking for a good manager, test another good manager and try to find a match trait-wise.

Some of the most popular personality tests are:

- Myers-Briggs Type Indicator (MBTI)
- DiSC® Assessment
- Caliper Profile
- California Psychological Inventory
- The Sixteen Personality Factor Questionnaire (16PF)
- The Minnesota Multiphasic Personality Inventory (MMPI)

Fees to administer the various tests range from a few bucks to several thousand dollars.

CHAPTER 8

FIND A WAY
TO SAY "YES"

Regardless of the kind of business you operate, your customers want only one thing from you: they want you to make their lives better. It's as simple as that. They have a problem that needs to be solved, and *it's your job to solve it*. This is the mindset you and your team need to have when going into any sales situation or any business consultation. Figure out what a customer's hot buttons are and what's driving them to come see you. Seek to understand exactly what it will take to make their life better, easier, and more efficient, and then find a way to say "yes." Dedicate yourself to meeting your customers' needs consistently, every time, whatever they might be.

WALK A MILE IN THEIR SHOES

Two of the best characteristics of people with A.D.D. are sensitivity and empathy. We are hard-wired to (1) pick up on how other people are feeling, (2) establish a connection with them around that feeling, and (3) respond accordingly. That's just the way we A.D.D.-types roll. Throughout my lifetime I've seen firsthand how my ability to connect with and react to others with compassion not only helps them but also myself. That's why I have always emphasized with my team that *empathy is the key to profitable growth*.

Here's what I mean: if a customer describes a problem or issue and you have too much of an internal or company-focused mindset, you immediately start thinking about what the issue means to *you*… how tricky the problem is for *you* to solve; how much time *you* are going to have to spend on it; which other people *you* are going to have to explain the situation to – in order to resolve it.

This attitude results in employees picking and choosing the work they do or don't want to take on – based on how difficult they perceive it to be, or how well-equipped they feel to tackle it. This is the opposite of having a customer-focused perspective. The bottom line is that if your people aren't saying "yes" often enough, money is walking out the door because of it.

The only thing your customer wants to hear from you is *"yes"* . . . as in, "yes we can." Obviously, you can't say "yes" to everything. If a customer asks for a 75% discount, you have my permission to respectfully decline. What I'm talking about here is having your default answer be in the affirmative. I'm talking about developing a positive approach. Starting with the philosophy that "there is always a way to say yes" forces you to take on the customer's perspective and set aside how their situation impacts you. Tell them "yes," and **then** you and your team can get to work figuring out how to resolve the situation.

People are willing to pay for "YES." Even if you don't have the core competency to say "yes" to something, do it anyway. This is when having a rock star team really pays off, because you need to be confident in their ability to make things work. For example, not many Lamborghinis came through Curry's Auto Service because there just aren't a whole lot of them around. Nor is there much information out there on how to fix them. But whenever somebody called in needing service for their Lamborghini, we said, "Yes, absolutely, we can fix it." Then we huddled up and figured it out. That led to even more Lamborghinis coming in, because Lamborghini owners in our area were desperate for a trustworthy, reliable, competent place to take their cars. We knew each Lamborghini that came into the bay was going to be worth *at least* a $5,000 ticket, so it was definitely worth it for us to dedicate the time and energy to learning how to work on them.

Therefore, if you're looking for a great way to set your company apart from the rest of the pack (and I know you are!), developing "a culture of yes" may be the magic bullet. Very few businesses have that philosophy, so let it be your competitive advantage. Just know that to carry out this strategy effectively, it's important to have both external and internal marketing campaigns to ensure that the customer-focus culture is being lived every day. It's not always easy to get your people to say "yes" to your customers consistently, but try it anyway, because the payoff can be substantial. Your A.D.D. gives you amazing powers of persuasion; this would be the perfect time to use them.

THE A.D.D. ENTREPRENEUR NEVER STOPS SELLING THE PHILOSOPHY

At Curry's Auto Service, we started out as a boutique shop building race cars and working mostly on European models. But as we grew to five and then ten stores, we had to become more mainstream and start working on *all makes and models* of vehicles. I wanted us to say "yes" to everything. To generate more traffic, we spent about half a million dollars on marketing and advertising per year to spread the good word about our services and our customer-focused philosophy. I also made a full-court press to improve our telephone etiquette. The telephone is the #1 tool in your toolbox. The purpose of the phone is to get customers in the door, so if your people aren't handling the phone correctly, they're taking money out of everybody's pockets. At Curry's Auto Service, each phone call we received was worth about $400 per car, so you'd better believe I wanted callers to be treated with the utmost respect. My goal was to make my folks the best in the business on the phone.

That's why I held frequent phone etiquette training, and I often recorded phone calls. That way I could hear with my own ears how our customers were being treated when they called our shops. Man, it used to drive me "freaking crazy" listening to the recordings and hearing all the ways we would say "no" to people. In one notable case, a customer called the shop at two o'clock on a Saturday afternoon.

"A couple of weeks ago, you guys told me I needed a power steering hose," the customer said. "I'd like to get that done."

"Great! When would you like to do that?" my employee asked.

"Well, I'd love to try and do it today."

And instead of saying, "Absolutely! C'mon down!" my employee sighed and said, "Sir, we are not microwaves. We don't offer instant gratification here."

I swear to you, I almost threw the phone across the room after hearing that. I'd just spent hundreds of thousands of dollars on marketing and advertising to get more customers in the door, and this was the way they were being treated when they called? After listening to the recordings for a few weeks and counting all the potential customers we had turned away, I calculated that we could have been working on an additional thousand cars a month had we been saying "yes" consistently!

We had to do something different, and quickly. In order to change my team's mindset, we launched an internal marketing campaign to sell the customer-focused philosophy to them. We had recently learned from our customer surveys and focus groups that the number one thing our customers wanted – before price, before honesty, before anything else – was *convenience*. They wanted their time back. They wanted to get in and out of the shop as soon as possible. The question then became: *How can we give them what they want? How can we make their lives better?* The answer: we can save them time. As it turned out, we were not in the car business, but the time business.

We decided that our internal marketing slogan was going to be, "Say Yes to an Hour or Less." We rolled that message out in each of our stores and began enforcing and reinforcing it, because as we learned in an earlier chapter, you can't just say something once and expect it to take hold. You have to repeat it over and over again to ensure it becomes part of the company culture. We put the slogan on our mouse pads. We hung up framed pictures of it. We had dozens of two-minute meetings about it. And it worked. "Say Yes to an Hour or Less" propelled us to the head of the class. It made us a ton of money. But even more importantly, it gave us a legion of happy customers who became enthusiastic ambassadors for our brand.

SAY "YES"... YOU NEVER KNOW WHERE IT WILL LEAD

I believe in the "say yes" philosophy so much that I made it a major part of my presentation to Sir Richard Branson and the other entrepreneurs assembled at Necker Island when I was there in 2014. At the conclusion of my talk, Branson was quick to point out that he had instilled the same mindset throughout the Virgin Group, where their internal marketing slogan was "The answer's yes – what's the question?"

As Branson and I both know from experience, customer focus is not just some New Age touchy-feely Kumbaya concept. It's the key to generating profit. So make it your business to find a way to say "yes", because you never know where it will lead.

For example, I'm not a techie, not by a long shot. But if I hadn't taken a leap of faith and said "yes" to hybrid battery conditioning technology, I would never have been able to launch my newest venture, **The Hybrid Shop**. Back in 2012, I met one of the world's leading technologists in all things hybrid, Dr. Mark Quarto. Mark worked at GM for 28 years as an Engineering Group Manager in Hybrid, Electric, and Fuel Cell Technologies. One of Mark's major contributions to GM was architecting the diagnostic systems for prototype and production advanced technology vehicles. In addition to engineering, Mark is a professional educator who has taught these advanced technologies at original equipment manufacturers (OEMs) and colleges and universities, in addition to other venues, throughout the world.

As if that weren't impressive enough, Mark is also an inventor who developed a way to condition used Nickel Metal Hydride (NiMH) batteries to about 95 percent of their original power and energy for around half the price of battery replacement. This technology not only saves the consumer money, but it's also better for the environment because nothing enters the waste stream, and no resources are needed to build a new battery.

Like I said, I met Mark and went to dinner with him and his wife, Chris, in Las Vegas in 2012. Chris' resume is just as impressive as her husband's. She has a Master of Science degree and worked in the international corporate world for thirty years. In 1987, she and Mark started their own company called Automotive Research and Design, or AR&D, which is the umbrella under which Mark invented his hybrid battery conditioning technology and training, among other things. When Mark and Chris retired from their day jobs a few years ago, they turned their full attention to running and growing AR&D.

Over dinner and a bottle of wine that night in Las Vegas, Mark and Chris told me about AR&D and the latest innovations in the hybrid world and described their hybrid battery conditioning technology to me. I have to admit that it was way over my head. Although we owned eight hybrids as customer shuttle and service vehicles at Curry's Auto Service, we didn't work on many of them at the time. Hybrids have a reputation for being difficult to repair. In fact, there's a big myth in the industry that working on hybrid cars is dangerous: that one slip up can kill you. In all honesty, we hadn't actively pursued that line of business. Still, I was fascinated by Mark's technology even though I didn't really get it.

Then I saw him speak the next month at an event in New Orleans, and we started talking again. Mark knew that we had some hybrid vehicles at Curry's Auto Service. He knew that we had some awesome technicians and that we were recently voted the #1 Auto Repair Shop in North America by *Motor Age* magazine. He offered to come in and give my guys two days of free training on his battery conditioning method. Even though I still didn't fully grasp Mark's technology, my A.D.D. curiosity was piqued. I said "yes".

In December 2012, Mark flew in to train my five best technicians and my store managers. It was awesome. I learned more about hybrid vehicles in the first three hours of that training than I had ever learned before. My technicians were super impressed, too. By the end of the first day, they were conditioning hybrid batteries. By the end of the second day, they were conditioning *and rebuilding* hybrid batteries. Mark left his equipment behind so we could continue to work on our vehicles. The results were astounding. Vehicles that were getting between 37 and 44 miles to the gallon before battery conditioning began racking up between 49 and 52 miles per gallon afterward. They also got all their torque back, restoring their acceleration and overall performance to optimum levels. I knew we were definitely onto something here.

Mark came back in January for the full four-day training. I had ten of my guys there, and they were blown away by the whole thing. Mark has his training program down to a science; it's a modular system with each section building upon the previous one. All of my techs said it was the best training they'd ever had. After only four days of training, my guys could condition batteries, replace motor generator units, repair inverters and converters... the whole nine yards. In short, we were able to diagnose, maintain, and repair everything on a hybrid vehicle.

January, February, and March passed, and we kept using the technology in our shop with awesome results. We were no longer afraid of hybrids. In fact, we were all stoked to be working on them. The truth is that there are so many safety redundancies built into hybrid vehicles, you have to be a complete idiot to get hurt.

I started giving this hybrid technology some serious thought. The way the auto industry is progressing, every auto repair shop is going to have to start servicing hybrid and electric cars eventually if they want to stay competitive. I saw enormous commercial potential in the technology, equipment, and training modules Mark and Chris had developed. After all, I figured that if Curry's Auto Service – the number one auto repair shop in North America with the best technicians on the planet – didn't know how to service hybrid vehicles, then probably most other shops didn't know, either. To me this was a huge opportunity for Mark, Chris, and I to build something *B-I-G* and share it with the world. By joining forces on this concept, they could concentrate on what they do best, which is R&D, training, technology; and I could focus on what I do best, which is branding, marketing, operations, and sales training.

So I went back to Mark and Chris Quarto and told them that I thought we could further commercialize this technology and training of theirs by turning it into a franchise model. I put together a business plan to bring their training, technology, and diagnostic equipment to market, and I got them to sign over the exclusive rights through licensing to support the franchise by distributing the AR&D equipment and training to automotive repair centers, shops, and garages throughout North America. We put the idea out there, and other shop owners and entrepreneurs were intrigued by it. A couple of months later we had 50 people fly in from all over the country to hear our pitch on what **The Hybrid Shop** is all about and to receive a free, one-day training. Four of those stayed on afterward to do the full four-day training. They loved it and became the original Hybrid Shop pioneers. We decided to ramp up and refine our vision, game plan, message, and marketing to take our franchise concept to the next level.

The Hybrid Shop was introduced to the masses in November 2013 at SEMA, the premier automotive aftermarket tradeshow in the world. Our booth was swarmed by thousands of people; we were overwhelmed with the reception we received. Within seven months of our debut at SEMA, we sold 31 franchises. At press time, we're in line to become one of the fastest growing franchises in North America.

And that's why I say that whenever somebody offers you an opportunity – inasmuch as it makes sense – find a way to say "yes," because you never know where it might lead. I look at it this way: if you want profitable growth and a legion of lifetime customers, you have to start somewhere, but I guarantee you won't get there by saying "no." You can be sure that if you don't say "yes" to your customers, someone else probably will.

GAINING TRACTION #6: A TIP FROM MATT

In the summer of 2014, my son Matt, Jr. and I traveled to Japan and Australia for a father-son adventure. We'd just finished taking a helicopter tour of Sydney and were sitting in the airport around 4:30 one afternoon waiting for our 8:30 p.m. flight to Brisbane when I noticed that our airline also had a 7:00 p.m. flight to Brisbane. By now you know me well enough to know that I hate to wait if I don't have to. So I checked online and found that there were seats available on the earlier flight, and I called reservations to see if we could switch. The representative said of course, but it would cost $250 per ticket to make the change. The tickets only cost $132 to begin with!

"Look," I said, "you've got plenty of empty seats on the seven o'clock flight. I'm already booked on your eight-thirty. How does it hurt your company to say yes and put us on the earlier flight for no additional charge? It's no big deal, right?"

Apparently it *was* a big deal because the representative put me on hold for 50 minutes. I hung up, walked down to the ticket counter, and explained the situation to the agent. She, too, insisted that I had to pay the change fee. I couldn't believe it. I decided to turn the experience into a teachable moment for my son, the budding entrepreneur. As we stood in front of the ticket agent, I turned to Matt and said, "Son, don't ever let your company's policies get in the way of customer service. Empower your people to make the right decisions to help your customers."

Long story short, the airline eventually came through and put us on the earlier flight for free. Still, the experience of being a paying customer and having to fight for such a simple thing left a really bad taste in my mouth.

GAINING TRACTION #6 (Cont'd....):

Don't let this happen to your business. Make sure your people know that they have full authority to say "yes" to take care of your customers at all times. Tell them that whenever they are faced with a situation like the one I describe above, they should ask themselves these three questions:

- **Is saying "yes" good for the customer?** Will this solve the customer's problem and make them feel good about us?

- **Is saying "yes" good for the company?** Does it benefit the company financially and strengthen our reputation for honesty and integrity?

- **Is saying "yes" good for me (the team member) personally?** Can I live with the decision? How would I feel if this were me? Will I feel that I have contributed to the bottom line for the company by satisfying this customer?

Only after they fully understand the problem and are able to answer these three questions in the affirmative can your people truly say "yes" from the perspective of truth.

CHAPTER 9

GUARD YOUR FINANCIAL REPUTATION

In a previous chapter I talked about how important it is for entrepreneurs to see around corners so we can properly execute our game plan, avoid hazards, and capitalize on the opportunities we're going to encounter along the way. In my view, the most basic tool for properly executing your business is your finances. Knowing how much money you have at all times, managing it well, and monitoring your company's financial reports and your personal credit rating… all are critical to your business success.

Most entrepreneurs claim to understand this, yet a significant percentage of startups fail each year because their owners run out of cash and can't get more. Obviously, some folks have not received the message about finances. As for me, I had a leg up when it came to money and financial analysis because of my A.D.D. superpowers. I absolutely love numbers. Math makes sense to me because there is only one correct solution. It is what it is. Either you made money last month, or you didn't. As a person with A.D.D., I dig that.

I also give credit to my mom for improving my ability to calculate and analyze numbers quickly. I once got into trouble at school for swearing, and to punish me, my mom made me learn the multiplication tables up to twenty, by heart. Every day I had to write them out. I'm not as good as I used to be at computing stuff in my head, but I can still multiply, divide, A.D.D., subtract, read financials pretty quickly to help predict the future (is it a train wreck or can it be salvaged?), and take quick decisive action to lead to a positive ending. That's A.D.D. That's Rain Man shit.

Don't despair if numbers are not your strong suit. Learn all you can, and then find a great and trustworthy financial guru to help you fill in the gaps. And read on for my best fiscal advice.

BUILD AND PROTECT YOUR CREDIT RATING

To borrow money, you have to be perceived as credible. Lenders and investors want to know they're dealing with a standup person who pays their bills on time. So when things are good and the cash is flowing, *that's* the time to establish your lines of credit. Don't wait until you are desperately in need of money, because that's the hardest time to get it. And don't go to one of the giant national banks. Go to a community bank, and build a relationship with a local banking professional who will advocate for you. It's *very* important to have one-on-one relationships with your bankers (and also attorneys, by the way). You don't want to be just a number to your banker. You want them to know you and trust you, because that trust will eventually pay off, big time. For instance, when we were growing, I had a relationship with a bank that financed *up to 125% of our operations!* That's practically unheard of in this day and age, but we were able to pull it off multiple times because the bank knew me and recognized that I was credit worthy and had good experience.

That's why I recommend instituting lines of credit early on with a local bank, and then use the credit even when you don't have to. This builds your credit history and demonstrates that you have a track record for handling finances responsibly.

Another reason to use your lines of credit periodically is to keep them open. You want to preserve your lines of credit for the long haul, because doing so raises your credit rating. If you don't use a line of credit, eventually the bank will shut it down. A bank can only lend four times the amount of money it has on hand. When you take out a line of credit and don't use it, the bank can't lend to and collect interest from another borrower. Consequently, they'll shut you down so they can free up that money for someone else, forcing you to have to reapply. Opening, closing, and applying for accounts too frequently will have an adverse effect on your credit rating. So establish a line of credit early, use it regularly and responsibly, and keep it open for as long as you can.

That's what I did, and it really paid off for me. Before I had Curry's Auto Service, I went into business with my best friend at the time. I'll call him Fred. I'd had my eye on a really nice repair shop that was for sale for $200,000, and I told Fred about it over a beer. He offered to go in on it with me. Fred had more money than I did, so we agreed that he'd put in $25,000 and I'd put in $5,000. Since I was the one with all the industry experience, I would be the managing partner and he'd be the silent partner, and we'd split the proceeds 50/50. Fred and I made an appointment with an attorney and told him what we wanted to do. The attorney said ours was the stupidest plan he'd ever heard. He actually wrote his thesis on all the reasons why people shouldn't enter into a 50/50 business. There are just too many pitfalls in that type of arrangement, he said. We swore that none of those risk factors applied to us. We were best friends. We'd known each other for years. No way would we ever have a problem. The attorney shrugged his shoulders, drew up the papers, and Fred and I bought the shop. We were in business.

When we took over, the shop had revenues of about $30,000 a month. Within eight months I had it up to almost $100,000 in monthly revenue. We were doing really well, but Fred and I started having disagreements. For example, Fred was supposed to help out in the shop one or two days a week, but he wasn't showing up at all. He wanted to collect a salary for doing nothing, while I wanted to use that money to pay for upgrades to our equipment. We couldn't see eye-to-eye on that and a few other things.

About nine months into the business, I took off one weekend and went to my parents' house with my family. I brought along my fax machine because I didn't want to miss anything at the shop (that's A.D.D. for you!). On Sunday, a fax rolled in: a memo stating that there was going to be a board meeting *that Monday* in which I would be kicked out of the company. Although our deal had been 50/50 ownership, Fred's position was that since he'd put in more money, he had control of the business… and he wanted me out.

When I got back to town on Monday, I found that Fred had changed the locks on the shop doors and taken away my access to the company's bank accounts. Even now, after all these years, it's painful recalling that experience. My whole freaking life had just exploded. All the blood, sweat, tears, and dreams I'd put into our business and our friendship… and it all came down to this? It was devastating. I contacted my attorney for advice about what to do. He felt sorry for me and gave me a huge break on his fee. He recommended we settle because fighting it out in court would be too costly and time consuming, and ultimately nobody was going to win. I agreed.

The kicker is that six months after my ouster, the shop went under. They had racked up a bunch of equipment loans; the business actually had a negative worth. And that brings me to the point of this story. Thanks to my excellent credit history and my fierce determination to save my financial reputation, I was able to get my name off of all the company's loans, keeping my outstanding credit rating intact. Had I not been able to do that, I doubt I would have been able to get Curry's Auto Service off the ground as quickly and successfully as I did soon afterward.

So listen up, because this is important: *a healthy credit rating is absolutely essential to your success as an entrepreneur. Build a strong financial reputation, and then guard it with your life. Let nothing – and I mean NOTHING – derail it.*

BECOME AN EXPERT ON FINANCIAL REPORTING

In order for you to see around corners and over mountains, your company must have a proper financial reporting system. From what I've seen, the majority of small businesses don't have much of any formal financial reporting except for maybe once a year in the form of a tax return. Consequently, from week to week or month to month, they have no idea if they're making or losing money. Their owners are flying by the seat of their pants. I understand that to a certain extent. Even for people without A.D.D., it's really hard to concentrate on projections, budgets, and P&Ls when you're trying to keep your head above water in the day-to-day craziness of running a business.

Still, that's no excuse. If you want your business to last, you must have some mechanism for generating an ongoing analysis of how you're doing so you can make timely adjustments. You need to have metrics and know what they are (your industry peers can help with this). You must have key performance indicators and track them on a daily, weekly, and monthly basis. That way, when you hit a rough patch, you'll get a quick heads up so you can intervene before it's too late. You can take control of the situation. Staying in the loop and taking control… that's what it's all about when you're a business owner.

One of the reasons Curry's Auto Service did so well for so many years was because we had a multi-tiered financial reporting system. Here's how it worked: I would receive a P&L on the 15th of each month detailing our expenses and revenue from the previous month. It was great information to have, and it was reasonably quick in coming, but still, two weeks is a long time in the fast-paced world of commerce. That previous month was history; I could have no impact on the past. As CEO, I needed to know where we stood on a daily and a weekly basis, too.

That's why we also had our managers generate daily and weekly worksheets we called Flash reports. These were a quick and dirty analysis of the previous day's or week's activity showing whether or not we'd made money and were on target for our goals in their particular store. If we weren't on target, the Flash reports helped the manager and I recognize it quickly so we could adjust on the fly. Let's say our goal was $50,000 for the first week of January, but the weekly Flash report showed we only did $40,000. Obviously we needed to make a correction in order to salvage the month and get to our profit. Maybe we'd cut payroll or do a special promotion for that store.

My point is that if you have to wait 15, 30, or 60 days to get your P&L only to discover that January really sucked, there's not much you can do with that information. It's past history. Flash reports help you deal with the here and now, while there's still time to make a positive impact. That's REALITY. That's dealing with the truth.

To summarize: do whatever it takes to become a financial whiz kid. One of the great things about having A.D.D. is that we're rarely intimidated by anything – even something as daunting as understanding corporate finance. So get out there and take some business and economics classes. Read everything you can get your hands on. Get a professional business coach. Learn to analyze financial reports. Build a solid credit history, and protect it at all costs. Hire a great accountant and bookkeepers, and set up a thorough financial reporting system. Train your managers to create daily and weekly Flash reports, and then personally read and analyze those reports. And never, ever take your eye off the fiscal ball.

GAINING TRACTION #7: A TIP FROM MATT

One of the best ways to protect your financial reputation is to make sure your credit reports are accurate. Credit reports include information about your bill paying history, where you live, how many accounts you have open, and whether you've filed for bankruptcy or been sued within the last few years. Lenders, potential employers, landlords, insurance providers, and others can buy your credit reports from any or all of the three nationwide credit reporting agencies (Equifax, TransUnion, and Experian) and use them to gauge your credit worthiness and overall dependability. That's why it's really important to examine your report periodically to (a) make sure that the information on it is accurate and (b) determine if your identity has been stolen.

The federal Fair Credit Reporting Act (FCRA) requires the three credit reporting agencies to give a free annual credit report to everyone who requests it. Visit www.annualcreditreport.com to order yours. Caution: do not be fooled by imposter websites that also claim to give you a "free credit report." There is always a catch. The URL above is the ONLY official site for receiving free credit reports as prescribed by FCRA.

CHAPTER 10

A.D.D. PIT STOP:
151 A.D.D. SUPERPOWERS

*I prefer to distinguish A.D.D. as attention
abundance disorder. Everything is just so
interesting... remarkably, at the same time.*

~ Frank Coppola

Even the most well-balanced A.D.D. entrepreneur can use a confidence boost now and then. That's why I love Adult A.D.D. Coach Pete Quily's list of *151 Positives of A.D.D.*[8] If I'm feeling down or otherwise need a shot of self-assurance, I can scroll through Pete's list and check off some of the helpful characteristics I possess – characteristics that have served me very well professionally and personally. Here are a few of my favorites:

- Ability to find alternate paths to overcome obstacles
- Adventurous, courageous, lives outside of boundaries
- Able to see the big picture
- Intuitive towards others' difficulties
- Can create order from chaos
- Energetic
- Fun person to be around
- Good at motivating self and others

---

8. http://www.addcoach4u.com/positivesofadd.html, accessed September 2, 2014.

- Has the gift of gab
- Impulsive (in a good way) not afraid to act
- Not afraid to speak mind
- Visionary

Focusing on my strengths helps put my "weaknesses" into their proper place. My deficits don't define me... and neither do yours. Check out Pete's list of 151 Positives of A.D.D., and make note of all the wonderful gifts your "disorder" has given you. Then use those gifts to DO ONE THING TODAY that puts you closer to your entrepreneurial goals.

CHAPTER 11

STOP CONFUSING AND START CONVINCING

Wouldn't it be great if there was a button you could push in the human brain that made people say "yes?" What if you could push that button with practically anybody, anytime, anywhere, and get them to buy your product or service? How awesome would that be?

Well, I'm here to tell you that there is such a button. There are certain words and phrases that are emotional triggers, and when people hear these words and phrases at the right time and under the right circumstances, it actually causes a chemical reaction in their brains that makes them more agreeable. Since our goal in sales is to direct people into agreeing with us and *getting them to say "yes"* to us as quickly as possible, understanding how to trip these triggers is important. If we can figure out what each individual customer's prime motivators are, we can use the emotional triggers to get them to decide to say "yes".

We have to keep things simple, though. Too much information slows down the decision-making process. When you start trying to dazzle a customer with bullshit, you are on your way to losing them. You have to make your sales pitch so straightforward that even a 12-year-old can understand it. This is one of those times when having A.D.D. is a real blessing. We are blunt; we are concise; and we're intuitive. We're able to get a quick read on what makes people tick, which makes it relatively easy for us to stop confusing and start convincing.

In this chapter, we are going to cover some of the attributes of a great salesperson, the art and science of selling, and sales as a process. Because just as auto technicians, lawyers, and doctors have processes, so do great salespeople.

THREE A.D.D. SUPERPOWERS THAT LEAD TO MORE SALES

Let's start with a quick experiment. Go into the bathroom, and look at yourself in the mirror right now. Then say out loud, "No." "Sorry." "We don't do that." "I can't help you." "That's impossible."

How did it look and feel when you said those words?

Now go back in front of the mirror and say, "Great!" "Super!" "Yes!" "Excellent!" "Awesome!" "No problem!" "I can do that!" "Love it!" "You 'da man!"

How did it look and feel when you said THOSE words? You couldn't help but smile by the time you were done, right? What a difference!

Just as it pained you to say the negative words and phrases, it also pains your customers to hear them. Those kinds of words and phrases do not inspire and motivate. They obstruct and deflate.

And that's why the number one attribute of a successful salesperson is a **great attitude**. Attitude is everything! The best salespeople are a blast to talk to. They know how to establish a rapport without being sleazy. They leave all their problems or worries at home and become like an actor on a stage when they're selling. They're not phony, though. In fact, it's just the opposite. They are the real deal. They're genuine, happy, positive, straightforward, and informative. They love what they do.

(Are you thinking what I'm thinking? Yes... all of the above describes most people with A.D.D.!)

Customers are drawn to salespeople like this. That's because they know how to forge a real connection with their customers on a person-to-person level. (More on forging connections in a moment.)

The second thing a great salesperson has is **confidence** – which is another A.D.D. trait. Effective salespeople believe in themselves and what they're selling. That kind of confidence comes from having product knowledge. I know I keep hammering on this over and over again, but it's only because it's so damn important. *You need to be an expert in your field and a master of the product or service you're selling*, whether you're selling auto repair, stereo equipment, cars, carpeting, IT services, shoes, barbequed ribs, pet supplies, or anything else. You need to know your product inside and out. People want to buy from someone who knows what they're talking about: someone who can show them the value of whatever it is they're buying.

So how do you get that kind of confidence? In the world of car racing, we call it *seat time*. The only way you can get familiar with a new racetrack is by spending time in the driver's seat, rolling around that track. The more you drive, the more you learn – about your car, the track, the conditions, the other drivers… and perhaps most importantly, about yourself. Confidence in racing comes from racking up real world driving experience. The same is true in sales. It's a fact that some of us are born with superpowers that make us great salespeople, but it's also a fact that anyone's salesmanship skills can be improved with study and regular practice. Make learning one of your life's goals. Make the investment of your time, energy, and resources in your particular field of expertise so that you can learn to solve other people's problems within that context. You just have to climb into the driver's seat every day and practice your pitches, because the more pitches you do, the more confident you become.

Lastly, to grow into a sales leader extraordinaire, you need to enter each sales situation **prepared**. Not only do you need to prepare yourself emotionally and mentally (with a positive attitude) and intellectually (with thorough knowledge of your products and the sales process) but also physically by having the proper tools and knowing how to use them. What props must you have on hand in your line of work? Is your paperwork within easy reach? Do you know how to use all of your company's technology, such as the software, the calculator, the cash register? You don't want your momentum broken by having to hunt for a pen or figure out the adding machine at the pivotal moment when you're trying to close a sale. Be a good scout, and be fully prepared to pitch and close a sale at a moment's notice. You have to be prepared for success!

THE FIVE C's OF SELLING

When you really stop and think about it, the art of selling is nothing more than the art of getting another person to do what you want them to do. The customer has a problem they need solved. You're trying to influence them into seeing your particular solution as the best one – the one that will make their life easier and better – thereby getting them to say "yes" to spending their money with you. The sales process is like a dance between you and the customer. Both of you are actively engaged, but if you do it correctly, you're the one leading the dance steps. To do that, you have to get to the core, to the meat of the matter, and trip the customer's emotional triggers as quickly as you can.

To guide my employees at Curry's Auto Service through the sales dance, I came up with a list of steps I call the Five C's of Selling, which I taught them in a series of training classes. The Five C's – **Commonality, Compliment, Connect, Collaborate, and Close** – build upon one another and make it easier to convert more sales. Let's walk through each one.

<u>**Commonality:**</u> As human beings, we like to be around people who are like us: people who share our interests and world view. Having things in common makes interactions between people easier and more pleasant for everyone involved. That's why we join civic groups, clubs, teams, churches, etc… and that's also why we prefer to do business with people we have something

in common with. Therefore, the most successful salespeople are always quick to spot and capitalize on the common threads between themselves and their customers.

For example, let's say I'm trying to sell you a set of tires. I see that you drive a minivan, and that there's an infant car seat strapped into a back seat. That means you probably have a kid. I have kids, too. *Voila!* Instant commonality. I can now say something like, "Hey, I see you have a child. That's great! I've got two kids myself. How old is your little one? Do you have a boy or a girl?"

Or maybe I see that you're driving a BMW. In that case I could say, "My best friend drives a BMW too, and he absolutely loves it. He says it handles like a dream. Are you happy with your car?"

Now, thanks to the commonality you've just established, you have a foundation upon which you can build. You're one step closer to making a sale.

Compliment: Not only do we like people who are like us, but we also like people who *like* us. When someone compliments us, we feel better about ourselves. We are happier. We feel smart, empowered, and more confident. A happy, confident, empowered person is more likely to say "yes" to a sales opportunity than an unhappy, insecure, discouraged person. Great salespeople are terrific at finding things about their customers that they can compliment, and they're also terrific at delivering those compliments in a genuine, heartfelt way. This is where people with A.D.D. really set themselves apart. We are super-observant, sincere, and naturally friendly.

When you're looking for something to compliment a customer, keep in mind that it doesn't have to have anything to do with the pending sale. All you're trying to do is make the customer feel good and to let them know that you like them. You can help them feel good (and smart!) by using affirmation phrases like, "I'm glad you mentioned that," or "Great point!" or "I'm really happy you asked about that, because..."

You can also say something like, "Mrs. Green, that bracelet is beautiful! It's a perfect match with your watch, too. You have exquisite taste." Now you've tripped an emotional trigger; your customer not only feels great about herself, but she's also more likely to do business with you *because* she feels great about herself. Win/win.

Connect: Once you've complimented a customer, the next step is to **weave that compliment into a story** that deepens the connection between the two of you and illustrates how your solution will solve their problem. Remember, the point of the sales process is to find out what motivates the customer and then use those motivators to have them take action and buy from you. You do that by connecting with them: by sharing a highly visual story that uses common sense terms they can understand.

"Wow, that's a really nice van, Mr. Anderson," you say. "When my kids were little I had a Caravan too, and it was probably the best car I've ever owned. I put Michelin tires on it because I wanted only the safest ride for my kids. I know you want the same thing for your kids, too. Come over here with me and let me show you the Michelins."

Or this: "Mr. Anderson, as you can see on this estimate, I'm recommending that you replace the timing belt right away, before it breaks. Another customer of mine had the timing belt break when his wife was driving their kids to an out-of-town soccer game, and they were stuck on the side of the road for hours. Not only that, but it bent the valves in the engine and ended up being a $4,000 repair. I'd really hate to see you and Mrs. Anderson have to deal with that kind of hassle and expense. So let's get this belt replaced right away. How about this afternoon?"

This is an example of what I call "YOU Messaging." YOU Messaging triggers brain activity, because – let's face it – we human beings are self-centered. When we're presented with a proposition, the only thing we want to know is "what's in it for me?" So connect with the customer by giving them what they want: **tell a story** that offers them a clear, vivid, graphic explanation of how your product or service will benefit them.

And then...

Collaborate: So far you've found and capitalized on a common thread between you and the customer. You've complimented them, and you've connected their specific need to your product through the use of a story. You've worked super hard to get the customer to see you as their ally, not their adversary. The time has come to really hammer it home by getting them to verbally buy into whatever it is you're recommending. You want to empower them to make a decision **now**. You do that by asking them affirmation questions such as:

- "Does that make sense?"
- "Does that sound good?"
- "Is that fair?"

If they say "yes" to your collaboration question, you can then proceed to the grand finale: the close. But should they raise an objection, don't give up. Address the objection and work to eliminate it. Think about it: objections are really just opportunities in disguise. Whenever a customer voices an objection, they are giving you a glimpse into their psyche and offering you important clues about their motivation in that moment. Take advantage of that opportunity!

Never forget that the customer is standing in front of you because they have a problem, and they came to you hoping you would solve it quickly and cost-effectively. They've given you a chance to be their partner. Work with them to overcome their objections. Reframe your solution. Then ask your collaboration questions again. Eventually your persistence will be rewarded.

Close: In any dialogue between two people, the person who is asking the questions is the person controlling the conversation. That's why it's so important to come right out and ask for the sale.

- *What time would you like to come in?*

- *What can I do to earn your business?*

- *How about I write up that order now?*

It's shocking to me how often salespeople skip this step and then wonder why their conversion rates are so low. If you've followed the other C's up to this point, the close should come naturally. There is nothing to be afraid of when it comes to closing the sale. Ask, and you shall receive.

THE SALES PROCESS IN SIX EASY STEPS

1. **Give a Friendly Greeting**: SMILE, even if you are only answering the phone. Be clear, patient, attentive, and professional. Get the customer's name, and write it down so you won't forget it. You'll refer back to it throughout the sales process.

2. **Understand the Need**: *Listen to their concerns and visualize their problem.* Ask qualifying, pertinent questions. Remember, the person who asks the questions controls the conversation. Use the customer's name. Validate their feelings. Connect to them and their world on a person-to-person level.

3. **Say "YES!"**: Respond to them with phrases like, "Great, we can take care of that." "Absolutely, we will handle that for you!" "Sure, we can do that. Our technicians are the best!" "No problem; I can look that up for you." "Definitely! When would you like to come in?" Again, use the customer's name.

4. **Make Specific Recommendations:** *Convince, don't confuse!* Keep it simple. Remember that too much information slows down the buying decision. Give the customer a set of "good, better, best" options. Mentally prepare to answer their objections. And of course… don't forget to call the customer by name!

5. **Explain the Benefits and Features:** *Use your product knowledge. Explain the value proposition.* Why should they choose you over a competitor? Explain what sets you apart,

keeping in mind the problem they've told you they want solved. Give them a picture in their mind's eye so they can clearly visualize and connect their problem to the solution you are offering. The fastest way to the brain is through the eyes. A picture really is worth a thousand words. Find a way to make your benefits tangible. Use emotional triggers to create a chemical reaction in the customer's brain. Make your solution so simple that even a child could understand it.

6. **Ask For the Sale!:** Assume the sale on every call, and sell with confidence. "When would you like to come in?" "I can get you in at three o'clock today, does that work for you?" Then *resell the solution* by confirming the product or service you're going to provide as well as the time and date of appointment, and make sure your customer knows where you are located and what the next steps are.

GAINING TRACTION #8: A TIP FROM MATT

The words you use when talking to a customer are important. They shape the tone of the conversation and have a direct bearing on the outcome of the encounter. Customers appreciate an honest, helpful, responsive, positive attitude – not a fake veneer of "yes." That's why it's important to choose your words wisely and practice your pitch so that using the right words becomes second nature.

In the training classes I gave to the Curry's Auto Service sales teams, I handed out lists of words that I've found helpful in my own sales situations over the past three decades. Some of these are what I call *attitude words* that convey a sense of positivity, cooperation, and goodwill; others I call *viscosity questions*, since they keep the conversation moving along.

So, without further ado, here are my lists of attitude words and viscosity questions. Feel free to use these words and questions to boost your own sales:

<u>Attitude words:</u>
- Awesome!
- Fantastic!
- Great!
- Fabulous!
- Nice!
- Warranty!
- We have the best people and equipment *in the industry*!

GAINING TRACTION #8 (Cont'd....):

- Easy!
- Convenient!
- No problem!
- Super-duper! (*My favorite.*)

...And some viscosity questions:

- Is that fair?
- How does that sound?
- When would you like to come in?
- What can I do to earn your business?
- Does that make sense? (*This is probably my favorite viscosity question.*)

CHAPTER 12

A PARTING SHOT

One of the coolest things about having A.D.D. is that I'm never without an idea for very long. Thoughts occur to me at warp speed, which is a constant source of entertainment for me. The downside of having rapid-fire thoughts is that it's hard to keep track of everything that enters my mind. That's certainly been the case as I've written this book. Now that we've almost made it to the end, I realize that I have a few more miscellaneous pieces of advice to share with you. So I want to spend our last few moments together tying up some of the loose ends.

PREPARE TO BE SUCCESSFUL

"Be Prepared" is not only a motto for Boy Scouts. It's also a great maxim for entrepreneurs, too. You want to be successful? You have to prepare for it. You have to lay the groundwork... physically, emotionally, mentally, and intellectually.

As we discussed a moment ago, to be physically prepared for success means to have all the tools of your trade at your disposal and in working order at all times. Make sure that every member of your team knows that you expect them to have their props ready, too. Customers don't want to have to wait while you fumble around trying to find a pen or a notebook or while you struggle to figure out the new computer system. Put some thought into your preparation at the start of each workday. If you think it would help you and your teammates to have a checklist for all the actual and/or intangible stuff that you need to have ready before opening the shop doors, make such a list, and require everyone to use it. That's what we did at Curry's Auto Service, and it really helped.

Another way for you and your team to be physically prepared for success every day is to create a set of formal processes and procedures. In my view, having written processes – and making sure everyone in your company knows that they are required to follow them – is one of the keys to success in business. At Curry's Auto Service, we worked very hard to develop standard processes to guide our employees because we knew that we would never be able to grow without them. Processes were what helped us standardize our customer experience no matter which employee was handling the intake or doing the work.

Without processes, companies become a messy set of tasks that are carried out depending on how each individual employee prefers to do them in any given moment. This is the opposite of building a consistent experience for all your customers across the board. Consistency is king, no matter what your industry might be. Consider McDonald's and Starbucks. Regardless of where you are in the industrialized world, you can rest assured that your McDonald's hamburger or your Starbucks latte is going to be exactly the same as the one you're used to getting back home. Consistency is comforting; it's what keeps us coming back for more. Customers don't like to be surprised, except maybe on their birthday. People *especially* don't appreciate surprises when it comes to spending their hard-earned money.

That's why we defined the exact steps we wanted our employees to go through every time someone brought a car into one of our shops. This was one of my A.D.D. obsessions. Our intake process called for the employee to interview the customer, visually inspect the car, review the vehicle's service history, look for alerts about recalls or other notices from the manufacturer, fill out all the accompanying paperwork, etc. We checked, double-checked, and triple-checked at every step along the way. Consequently, very few things fell through the cracks at Curry's Auto Service. Our customers loved how methodical and thorough we were, which brought us tons of repeat business and referrals.

Having made the point about how important process was for us at Curry's, I'm now going to tell you about one of our team members who took it upon himself to ignore our customer intake process. And, of course, it came back to bite us... hard. This particular Curry's employee was wrapping up a visit with one of his friends outside the shop one day after a meeting. While saying their goodbyes near the friend's car, the Curry's team member noticed that one of his friend's tires was low. So he said something like, "Hey, let me pull your car into the shop, and we'll take a look at that tire for you." No intake process, no check-in paperwork, no visual inspection. Nobody interviewed the guy to find out about the car's history, or his driving habits, or to research the vehicle's service records. Nothing... just bring her on in!

Once the car was inside the bay and up on the lift, our technician saw that the low tire had a nail in it. But he also discovered that all of the tires were nearly bald and the car needed alignment. When he removed the tires, he saw that the front and rear brakes were worn out and needed to be replaced. Last but not least, the vehicle was overdue for an oil change. The estimate for doing the work came in at $4,500.

Being a good guy, our Curry's team member offered his friend his own personal car while the friend's car was in our shop. Is that our standard written process? Of course not! But process had been tossed out the window a long time ago.

And that's not the end of it. Unfortunately, this was one of those situations that compounded itself exponentially. The vehicle in question was a very high-end, sophisticated V12 European model, a somewhat over-engineered (and therefore, fairly cantankerous and expensive) car, which led to further issues being uncovered. During the technician's test drive after doing the brake and tire work, a series of warning lights came on indicating problems with the anti-lock brake system and the engine. Because we hadn't followed proper procedure by interviewing the customer and test driving the car *before* we started working on it, we didn't realize that it had several additional and rather significant problems.

The bottom line is that had we adhered to our standard written processes, we would have been able to give an accurate up-front estimate of about $10,000 to repair that car. But by skipping the visual inspection, test drive, and customer interview (as well as many other critical steps and procedures along the way), we only "found" $4,500 worth of work. What would have been a nice opportunity to generate a tidy profit ended up costing me almost $6,000, because I insisted that we do the right thing and honor our original estimate. But boy, was I mad!

I don't usually do this, but I am now going to call out the guilty Curry's employee by name.

It was… Matt Curry.

That's right, folks. It was me – Mr. Process himself. I'm not even going to try to offer an excuse for my lapse in judgment, except maybe to blame it on my A.D.D. I tend to want everything done NOW. When you're a leader, it's crucial to create a sense of urgency, but you still have to follow your processes and procedures. We'd put so much time, effort, and creative destruction into making our processes the best in the business, and then I was the one to drop the ball! What a great (albeit expensive) lesson I learned. The next time I wanted to help a friend, you can be darn sure I followed our standard procedures!

I recommend that you do the same. Always. No exceptions. Develop sound policies and procedures, and teach them to your people. Remember to enforce and reinforce. Hold lots of two-minute meetings. Don't turn any employee loose with your customers until you're sure they're fully prepared to toe the line. And above all else, make sure that you practice what you preach, because how can you expect your people to follow the rules if you don't? Set a proper example.

Preparedness extends beyond the nuts and bolts of having sufficient supplies, putting sound written policies and procedures into place, and training your people to use them every time. You also have to prepare yourself mentally and emotionally for success. I'm a firm believer in the power of positive thinking. One of the reasons I've had this much success in business is because I knew deep down in my soul that I was going to make it happen, A.D.D. or no A.D.D. I'm not talking about simply having the faith that you might succeed. I'm talking about **KNOWING BEYOND THE SHADOW OF A DOUBT** that you will triumph, no matter what... that you will knock down every wall... that you were born for this – you were born to have this business and this lifestyle you are imagining for yourself and your family. In all honesty, I'm not sure it's possible to go very far as an entrepreneur without that kind of conviction.

That's because running a business is tough, man. It's tough on you, and it's tough on your family. Even when things are going well, it can still take a toll on your health, your finances, and your peace of mind. Steel yourself for that. Prepare yourself mentally and emotionally, like a gladiator getting ready for battle. Convince yourself that you've got what it takes to overcome whatever obstacles you might encounter along the way and that your "flaws" are what set you apart from the pack and make you stronger. Surround yourself with smart, positive, trustworthy people who support you one hundred percent – people who believe in your vision wholeheartedly. Fake it 'til you make it. Behave as if you've already hit the big time. And above all, know that *you deserve to have your dreams come true.*

ALWAYS BE INTERVIEWING

Like many other businesses in the service industry, the automotive repair business is plagued with a high turnover rate. As the old saying goes, tool boxes have wheels for a reason. Regardless of your industry, if, despite your best efforts, you make a bad hire – you bring in someone who causes stress in your culture, is dishonest, does consistently sloppy work, or has an attitude problem – cut your losses and cut those ties. Don't waste another minute of your time or another ounce of energy on them. Frankly, I would rather work shorthanded than subject myself and my team to such a person.

If the thought crosses your mind that perhaps you should fire someone, even if it's just a fleeting thought, pay attention. Your gut is trying to tell you something. I subscribe to the Jack Welch School of Management. Welch was the CEO of General Electric for over twenty years, throughout the 1980's and 1990's. He came up with a management system he called "Differentiation," but a lot of other people call it "Rank and Yank." The way it works is that you evaluate your employees and divide them into three categories as follows: 20% excellent, 70% average, and 10% below average. Then you sit down with every one of your people on an individual basis and let them know where they stand. You give nice incentives to your top 20%. You encourage your mid-range people to improve (and provide them with the tools and training to do so). And you get rid of the bottom 10%. Out the door they go. Then every year you rank your people again, and you eliminate the bottom 10%. And so on. Lather, rinse, and repeat.

Welch's system may sound harsh, but it works. I've fired hundreds of people over the years. I'm not proud of it, but it was efficient. In fact, I advocate taking Welch's system a step further and firing the bottom 20% every year. I believe such drastic measures are necessary sometimes, because we business leaders tend to promote people beyond their level of competence. Whenever we do that, it's our duty to acknowledge it and fix it right away before it drags down the company and our other team members. Sometimes we have to hit the reset button repeatedly in order to set things straight, but that's our responsibility as leaders. We have to suck it up and shoulder the load, even though that load can get very heavy and difficult to bear sometimes.

LISTEN TO YOUR MOM

It doesn't matter how grown up you are, or how much amazing stuff you've seen and done in your life. As long as you do the things your mom taught you when you were a kid, you'll come out on top every time – especially in all the ways that matter most. That's why I always told my employees at Curry's Auto Service this: if you want to have a happy life and a successful career here at Curry's, just follow your mom's teachings. Share your toys. Open doors for people. Give up your seat to someone in need. Don't litter. Say "good morning," "please," "thank you," and "excuse me." Be fair. Be honest. Clean up after yourself. Take responsibility for your actions. Stand up for what you believe in. Apologize when you hurt someone. Be grateful for everything you have. Live within your means. Serve others. And above all, *be yourself.*[9]

That last one – *be yourself* – can be tough for people with A.D.D. Many of us have a hard time with social skills and forming and maintaining relationships. We blurt out answers before the question is finished, and sometimes we say inappropriate things at inappropriate times. We talk excessively, and we interrupt conversations. I use this "ailment" as a "No Bullshit" superpower to give honest feedback and constructive criticism. Since I recognize that I sometimes talk too much and dominate the room, I make a conscious effort to listen more. In social situations, I try very hard not to interrupt. But when I do, I try to say something relevant, and when I blurt out inappropriate things, at least I try to make them funny. So be yourself, but begin each day with the goal of being a better version of yourself than you were the day before.

There's one final thing our moms taught us that I want to bring up here: *DO THE RIGHT THING!* At Curry's Auto Service, we donated our time, talent, and equipment to fix cars for homeless people and vans for churches. We gave vehicles to charity.

---

9. Even though my A.D.D. made me a challenge sometimes, my mom ALWAYS encouraged me to be myself. Thanks, Mom!

We started a youth sports league so neighborhood kids and their families would have fun, healthy things to do after school, on weekends, and during summer vacation. We covered the sides of ugly buildings with beautiful art the whole community could enjoy. We were determined to do the right thing. We were determined to get to *"yes"*. That's what a problem-solving solution-driver does. How do you get to "yes"? You find out what the opportunities are in your community. You figure out how you can make things better, and then you step up and do it. It's as simple as that.

All these mom-isms are universal for a reason. They actually work. They help us get along with other people as individuals, and they help us function as part of the collective good, which I believe is essential to being happy and successful in life. Being happy and successful for any length of time takes hard work. It doesn't just magically happen to people; you have to put a lot of thought and effort into it. So do what I've always tried to do in both my personal and professional lives, and follow Mom's advice every day. Excellent things will come of it. I guarantee it. If nothing else, you'll go to sleep each night feeling good about yourself... and nothing can top that.

GAINING TRACTION #9: A TIP FROM MATT

By now it ought to be pretty clear that I'm all for recognizing and leveraging your unique superpowers, whatever they might be. Identify them, celebrate them as gifts from God, and use them to make your life, business, and community better. I believe that's our responsibility as human beings and as entrepreneurs.

I believe it is also our responsibility to take it a step further and motivate other people – especially those with A.D.D. – to find and use their superpowers, too. Help your partners, associates, and employees uncover their unique gifts, and inspire them to put those gifts to their best and highest use both inside and outside your company. Not only will your business be better for it, but you'll also have the satisfaction of paving the way for the people around you to be their best superhero selves, to be accepted for who they really are… to make it possible for them to live their most genuine, profound truth.

Come to think of it, that may be the greatest superpower of all.

ACKNOWLEDGMENTS

I would like to thank my beautiful wife, Judy, for all of her love, loyalty, and dedication through the chaos I bring into her life. Her unwavering support has allowed me to take risks that many other relationships would not have been able to survive. Entrepreneurs can create a lot of disruption, stress, and financial upheaval in their relationships, but Judy has always supported all of my A.D.D. endeavors without fail. I could not have asked for a better partner in life and in business.

I would like to thank our kids, Matt Jr. and Jenna, who put up with my craziness and who have grown up to be fine young adults of whom I am very proud.

Great thanks and much love go to my Mom and Dad and my entire family for the sound upbringing based in love, a strong work ethic, honesty, and integrity. All six of my brothers and sisters remain very close to this day, and that's an accomplishment in itself. They have each supported me and my family through the best and the worst of times.

Sincere thanks to my in-laws, Tom and Nancy Bender, for believing in me and giving me a loan to start Curry's Auto Service.

Thank you to my long list of friends. All of you have blessed my life and brought me many great times, much fellowship, and laughter.

I want to thank Jody Ruth, my valued and trusted advisor. Also profound thanks to Mark and Chris Quarto. Without their technical expertise and professionalism, my latest venture, **The Hybrid Shop**, would not exist.

Thanks to Yanik Silver, leader of *Maverick Mayhem*, for all the great adventures, and to Derek Coburn of Cadre and all my Maverick and Cadre DC friends and fellow entrepreneurs. I extend much gratitude to Cameron Herold for writing the foreword to this book. Cameron, your books and your philosophy make the world a better place, and your teachings inspired me to write this book. Thanks to Bob London for your friendship, advice, and for your input on the book. I also want to thank Richard Branson for sharing his life experiences with me and for welcoming me to Necker Island and also to his lodge in South Africa.

Very special thanks to Nick Bruno, Co-founder of DSYS, Steve and Lori Bell, Dave Hindrich, George Collins, Ron Masci, Kelly and Gus Dipierro for helping to start and run DSYS. Also, I would like to thank all the Curry's Auto Service employees and Vernon Abel.

Sincere thanks to Nick Nanton, Angie Swenson, and all the other fine folks at Celebrity Press for helping me make my publishing dreams come true. And thank you, Pamela Suárez, for helping me to write this book and for being so patient in dealing with my A.D.D.!

And finally, to all the Curry's Auto Service customers out there: thank you for your business and for your trust. It was truly an honor to serve you.

ABOUT THE AUTHOR

Matt Curry has worked in the automotive aftermarket business for over 30 years. He started changing tires when he was 15 and worked his way into management, overseeing seven automotive stores for several different companies, doubling and tripling sales and profits at every store he managed.

In 1997, Matt and his wife, Judy Curry, started Curry's Auto Service with one shop in Chantilly, Virginia. Curry's Auto Service ultimately became one of the largest independent auto repair chains in the Washington, DC metro area, with nine shops across Northern Virginia and one in Maryland. Matt and Judy succeeded in differentiating Curry's from its competitors by offering strong value propositions that highlighted under-represented demographics within the auto repair industry. By instituting prominent eco-friendly, green-focused programs and community outreach, and earning female-friendly accreditation from AskPatty.com, Curry's actively contributed to the economic, social, and environmental development of the communities in which it operated.

In 2010, Curry's was chosen by the readers of Northern Virginia Magazine as the "Best Auto Repair Shop" in Northern Virginia. That same year, Curry's was named *Motor Age* magazine's Top Shop in North America. In 2011, the company was awarded the prestigious Angie's List Super Service Award and voted Top Shop Finalist by *Tire Review* magazine. Matt was also recognized as a "Home Grown Hero, Entrepreneur of the Year" by The Network for Teaching Entrepreneurship.

During the recession in 2008 and through 2011, Matt launched a major expansion, growing from four stores in 2008 to nine in 2011. In recognition of this growth, Curry's was named to the Inc. 5000 list for 2009, 2010 and 2011, moving up about 1000 spots each year. Curry's opened its tenth store in March 2013.

In addition to being an Inc. 5000 company for three consecutive years, Curry's was ranked the 126th fastest-growing business in Consumer Products and Services Industries by *Inc.* last year. Curry's was also recognized as one of the 50 fastest-growing companies in the DC region by both the *Washington Business Journal* and *Washington Smart CEO*.

In early 2013, Matt expanded his business model, investing in two vertical companies: a computer development company and a technology company called **The Hybrid Shop**, which specializes in electric vehicle propulsion systems. After only 12 months, in November of 2014 **The Hybrid Shop** successfully raised $2.5 million through a PE raise.

Matt and Judy made a successful exit from Curry's Auto Service by selling to a publicly-traded, $1 billion corporation in August, 2013. They now concentrate full time on **The Hybrid Shop**, the world's leader in training and education in the diagnosis, maintenance, and repair of hybrid vehicle technology and battery conditioning and repair.

COMMUNITY SERVICE AND AWARDS

In 2004, Matt raised $209,000 and launched the Dulles South Youth Sports (DSYS) league in August of 2006. More than 1,600 area children and teens now participate in the DSYS leagues each year. The Currys continue to advise the organization and help fund DSYS needs, including starting a scholarship and field fund in the hope that DSYS will have its own private playing field someday.

In 2012, Curry's Auto Service was a finalist for the Washington Area Jefferson Awards for Public Service. Matt and Judy have donated their time and money, totaling over $500,000 to 57 national and regional charitable groups, churches, parent-teacher associations, and youth athletic clubs since they started their company in 1997 and were recognized by *The Washington Business Journal* in 2012 as among the region's Top 50 Corporate Philanthropists.